Florence Marryat

Véronique

Vol. I

Florence Marryat

Véronique
Vol. I

ISBN/EAN: 9783337052225

Printed in Europe, USA, Canada, Australia, Japan

Cover: Foto ©ninafisch / pixelio.de

More available books at **www.hansebooks.com**

A Romance.

BY
FLORENCE MARRYAT,
(MRS. ROSS CHURCH,)
AUTHOR OF "LOVE'S CONFLICT," "NELLY BROOKE," ETC.

> "Man's love is of man's life a thing apart,
> 'Tis woman's whole existence."
>
> — BYRON.

IN THREE VOLUMES.
VOL. I.

LONDON:
RICHARD BENTLEY, NEW BURLINGTON STREET.
1869.

[All rights reserved.]

TO

CHARLES DICKENS, ESQ.

"My Dear Sir,

"I thank you sincerely for permitting me to write your name upon the dedication page of 'Véronique.' My offering is but a common flower—perhaps a weed—but, at any rate, plucked freshly from the fields of my imagination; and neither forced in a hot-house, nor sprung from a dunghill, as some of the criticisms upon modern novels would lead one to believe. 'Véronique' will not live longer than a gathered blossom, but whilst she does so I lay her at your feet, with greater pride in the remembrance that you were one of my dead father's nearest friends, than that you are the greatest living novelist of the age.

"Believe me,

"With every kind regard and wish,

"Sincerely yours,

"Florence Marryat Church."

Brussels, May, 1869.

PREFACE.

TO THE NOVEL-READING PUBLIC.

ALTHOUGH my name has been now for more than four years your common property, to praise or censure as you please, I have never yet ventured to appear before you in my proper person, or speak a word upon my own behalf; nor should I intrude myself upon your notice even now, did not the plot of "Véronique" call for a brief explanation.

The word "sensational" has been so twisted from its original meaning by the cant of what, in this age, we term criticism, that it has become difficult to know in what sense it should be applied. To affirm that the story I submit to your approval is not sensational, *i.e.*, that its incidents are not intended to appeal to your feelings, would be erroneous, since it boasts no higher claim; but on the other hand, should I be accused of distorting nature in order to give birth to a "monstrosity of fiction," my answer is, that the most unlikely scenes depicted here, the adventures on the Neilgherry Hills, and the wreck in the Chinese seas, have happened, and are drawn from life; and it is a remarkable fact, that those incidents in my novels which have incurred most abuse or ridicule at the hands of the public press, have invariably been those gained from the same source. The situations which I create are passed as probable; those which I have seen take place, rejected as libels against nature. To quote an abler authority than myself :—" Whenever you present the actual simple truth, it is somehow always denounced as a lie; they disown it, cast it off, throw it on the parish; whereas the product of your imagination, the mere figment, the sheer fiction, is adopted, petted, termed pretty, proper, sweetly natural; the little spurious wretch gets all the comfits, the honest lawful bantling all the cuffs." Perhaps my honest bantling may share the same fate, but I attest his legitimacy before the world.

I perfectly agree with the following sentiment, as delivered by the Saturday Review, on the ninth of last January:—" Let a man once have absolute confidence in his line, whether of thought or action, and he smiles at attack." And I have proved it by carrying out this tale to its legitimate conclusion, in spite of the onus which will probably accrue to me.

But a novelist is professedly a delineator

of human nature, and I maintain that whilst half the world sits in mourning, a true craftsman has no right to paint life one clash of marriage bells. He has no right, in fact, to deny the instinct which is in him, and will make itself heard, since, strive as he may, his best achievement must fall so far short of his lowest ambition, in order to bring his novels up (or down) to the standard of the circulating libraries. And for my own part, ephemeral as are the secondary romances of the present day, I have sufficient reverence for the profession of which I know myself to be so unworthy a disciple, to make me prefer that my efforts should fall stillborn from the press, rather than flourish by pandering to a false taste for falser art. Notwithstanding which avowal, I venture to hope that "Véronique" may be received with no less kindness than her predecessors, and I gladly take this opportunity of thanking you, who are my true critics, (and the only critics whose opinions make or mar my fortune), for the cordial hand-grasp which from the first you have stretched forth to me, and which, (though doubtless in a great measure given for my father's sake), has had more than the power to counterbalance such small disagreeables as a woman placed in my position must inevitably incur.

FLORENCE MARRYAT CHURCH.

CONTENTS OF VOL. I.

CHAPTER		PAGE
I.	ON THE BLUE MOUNTAINS	1
II.	THE MISSIONARY'S FAMILY	20
III.	THE AVALANCHE BUNGALOW	42
IV.	LOST AMONG THE PRECIPICES	63
V.	PERE JOSEPH	86
VI.	ON THE TRACK OF THE TIGER	108
VII.	AN AWKWARD TUMBLE	130
VIII.	SAINTE VERONIQUE	154
IX.	THE PROSTRATE A.D.C.	173
X.	A TOUCH OF THE GREEN-EYED MONSTER	192
XI.	THE OOTACAMUND POST-OFFICE	215
XII.	"ERIN" AMONGST THE TODAHS	239
XIII.	MONSIEUR! JE NE PEUX PAS	259
XIV.	GORDON ROMILLY'S DECISION	280
XV.	HONEY VERSUS MONEY	303

VÉRONIQUE.

CHAPTER I.

ON THE BLUE MOUNTAINS.

On the blue mountains! What pleasant memories does not the phrase recall. The vision of a lofty ghaut with tropical vegetation clinging about its steep and rugged sides, up which the straining oxen labour painfully, stopping to breathe at every twenty paces, little recking the while that their cloven feet are trampling down a bed of flowers, which conveys no idea of rest or beauty to their wearied senses.

The vision of bright waters: some, leaping in foaming wrath from one mountain's ledge to another, dashing their frothy spray around them as they fall, and emitting a never-ceasing roar, which may be heard for half a mile away; others dripping noiselessly from rock to rock, and quietly trickling over their time-worn courses—furrows in the cheek of mother Earth—as though Nature's sluices were open, and she were weeping silently over the little notice taken by man, of her exceeding beauty.

The memory of eleven miles of romantic tangled loveliness, but every step of which is a wearisome ascent, until the traveller stands on table-land once more, and turning to survey the mountain he has left behind him, finds that the snowy clouds are lying beneath his feet, hovering half way down the ghaut which he has just ascended.

Up in the clouds! what kind of country can this cloud-land be? A belt of hills, verdant everywhere, except where the pathways are cut, like deep scars upon their broad, green breasts, and in the valley formed by their magic circle, a wide, calm lake, across the centre of which, a bridge connects the two sides of the English settlement, known by its native name of Ootacamund.

Dark fir-trees, standing out in bold relief against the clear blue sky, and white châlet-looking houses nestling in their bowery gardens against the sides of the hills, remind the stranger at a first glance of Switzerland; the church with its tall spire topping the umbrageous trees, and the roses, geraniums and heliotropes, with which even the hedges are lined, carry his thoughts back to old England; whilst the dirty native huts, huddled about the margin of the lake, recall his mind at once to the fact that he can be nowhere but in the tropics.

Yet that vast range of undulating hills which meets his eye on every side, rising smoothly one above another like waves upon a summer ocean, and stretching far out into the distance, until the naked sight can follow them no longer; to what country, if not to cloud-land, can they belong? Hills upon hills—vapoury—undefiled and yet existent; the majority of which have never, to European knowledge, been trodden by the foot of man; whose echoes have never resounded to the gossip of camp scandal or the whisper of unlawful wooing; the pure and undefiled amongst the Neilgherries. There they lie—no one peak particularly surmounting another in height, but forming an interminable vista of hill and valley; mist-crowned top and sheltered sholah; each mountain a great possession in itself of probably fertile ground, and certainly never placed there with the intention of remaining uninhabited and unused.

As the eye roves over them, bathed in the soft smile of moonlight, or laughing in the brighter glories of the sunshine, and the mind remembers that, save for the sustenance of the samba, ibex, and wild buffalo, and the protection of the cheetah, tiger, and bear, they are useless, it naturally reverts to the numbers of unhappy wretches who lie festering in our London courts and alleys; who die by hundreds, weekly, of disease induced by starvation and foul air; and sighs to think how easy it is to plan, how hard to do!

Is it impossible that a possession of such magnitude, and the pure and bracing atmosphere of which has rendered it the most famous of our sanatoriums in the East, could be utilised for the benefit of those thousands who might emigrate with advantage to their country and themselves?

But it is less trouble to bury them after all, and whilst Government is considering the matter, their great great grandchildren will have had ample time to be pulled up, and pulled down, in like manner with themselves.

Beyond a few miles' circuit of the three English settlements, Ootacamund, Coonoor, and Jackatella, the Neilgherry hills are unknown territory, and will probably remain so to all time; for even the aboriginal Todahs, though they retreat yearly as the progress of civilization encroaches on their villages, are too much alive to their own interests to separate themselves entirely from the more fortunate people who have usurped their native soil.

Their maunds are always erected within

a convenient distance of the cantonments, and the droves of fierce-looking buffaloes, from the produce of which they derive their chief support, may be met, with lowered horns and threatening attitudes, on every mountain path.

If Todahs ever think, I wonder with what kind of feelings they regard the careless equestrians, who, jesting, and flirting, and making merry with each other, canter round the lake each evening; who fill the houses they have erected on the spot where Todah maunds once stood, with laughter, mirth, and feasting; who call Ootacamund their property, and have rebaptised it in their own language; and who pass them by, the true lords of the soil, with a look either of indifference or disdain—if they honour them with a look at all.

Marius weeping over the ruins of Carthage could not make a grander picture, than the portraiture of one of these poor Todahs as he stands, gazing with proud melancholy at the altered aspect of his country; his only covering, the wide blanket cast round him like a Roman toga, concealing a form as fine in its proportions as its height; whilst his dark face, with its deepset eyes, Jewish features, and curled Assyrian beard, expresses but too plainly what his tongue has neither the courage nor the power to reveal.

But the Neilgherry Hills are not Carthage, and our innovations have very much improved the appearance of the place, and ought to, if they have not, increased the felicity of its first inhabitants, therefore it is useless saying anything more about it. Besides, the Todah has one resource left him, denied to his European brethren; if he does not like the situation or his neighbours, he can always "move on."

* * * * *

It was about four o'clock in the afternoon, and the Neilgherry sun, which, at its meridian, is generally too powerful to render walking a pleasure, was beginning to cast long shadows on the grass, and show symptoms of decline, when a young man, fashionably dressed in morning attire, appeared in the doorway of the reading-room of the Ootacamund club, and stood on the threshold, leisurely examining the occupants of the apartment.

In age not over four-and-twenty; fair, well-featured, and above the middle height, his appearance was decidedly *distingué:* but the full, bright blue eye betokened a want of power in his reasoning faculties, and the retreating mouth and chin (although this latter defect was nearly concealed by the large moustaches and whiskers which he wore) a corresponding want of decision in his character.

That he was a stranger there, was evident, by the cool indifference with which he returned the inquisitive glances directed to his figure, from above every newspaper and magazine in the room, and the motionless attitude he retained upon the threshold, as though he were attentively scrutinising a collection of curious animals.

Until, indeed, a cheery voice from the other end of the apartment, exclaimed:

"Gordon Romilly! as I'm a living sinner!" and a man, some years his senior, capsizing his chair, in the excitement of the discovery, rushed forward to greet him with extended palm. Some sort of interest did seem to light up Captain Romilly's handsome, passive countenance, at the sound, and he appeared almost as pleased as his friend, as he gave vent to the response.

"Romer! by all that's sacred! Why, who on earth would have dreamt of meeting *you* here?"

"I might put the same question to yourself. I knew you were in India, of course, but thought you would have had too much duty on your hands to permit of your leaving Madras. When did you arrive?"

"This morning!"

The words were dragged out slowly, and with a peculiar intonation, as though the speaker were articulating from the back of his throat—Captain Gordon Romilly being one of those young gentlemen of the modern time, who consider it the correct thing (when in society at least) to appear so utterly fatigued with the mere fact of existence, that they are not even equal to the exertion of speaking plainly. His manner, in this respect, was a great contrast to that of his friend, who was a bluff, hearty Englishman, talking, perhaps, a trifle too loudly, but never guilty of saying a word of which he had need to be ashamed.

"What an age it seems since we parted!" said Captain Romer; "why I don't think you had doffed jackets, Romilly, when I said good-bye, to the dear old College; and now we have met on the Neilgherries! What brings you here, old fellow! not ill health, I hope?"

"Want of change, my dear Romer! I've been sick of my life ever since I landed in this detestable country."

"Tired of it already," exclaimed the other, "and you have not been in Madras three months?"

"Three months! I beg your pardon,

but have you ever been quartered in the place you mention?"

"I should think I had—for three years, and only took sixty days' leave during the whole time."

"Indeed! Well, I wonder you're alive to tell the tale."

"Why, what has the old town been doing to fall into such disfavour with you?" asked Captain Romer.

By this time every ear in the reading-room was pricked up to listen to the conversation passing between the two young men, and eyes were beginning to glare at the turn that it was taking.

"Doing, my dear Romer," was Captain Romilly's sarcastic expostulation, "I wish to heaven it had been doing anything, but, as far as I can judge, it has done nothing at all ever since I was unfortunate enough to place my foot in it."

"No balls—no dinners—or parties of any sort?"

"I have been to one or two entertainments, at which people have attempted to dance; and where, after the first half-hour, the men's shirt-collars have laid down like lambs, and the women's faces have been something too horrible even to think of. But I have taken good care never to try anything of the kind, myself,"—and here Captain Romilly made such a comical gesture of disapprobation that Captain Romer laughed.

"But they give good dinners there, at any rate."

"Very good, doubtless, if one had the chance of tasting them; but with this new system of serving dinners, *à la Russe*, and confiding the carving part of the business to natives, the most I have ever succeeded in obtaining was a cold cutlet, or the drumstick of a turkey, just as the second course was being handed round, so that I am not in a position to testify to the excellence of their dinners."

"And yet you must have been in the way of seeing the best of them, Romilly."

"I daresay I have!"

"And have not a word more to say in their praise than this?"

"Oh! excuse me—the champagne is excellent, and Bass knows what he is about when he bottles the beer for this country, else I really don't believe I should have survived it so long."

"You look in very good case, nevertheless, and you have come to the very place to put you in still better. But what about the ladies, Romilly—have you done any damage amongst them?"

At this query, perceiving the eyes of the whole room fixed upon him, Captain Gordon Romilly feigned total inability to understand.

"Excuse me!"—

"Didn't you lose your heart to any of the Madras beauties?" repeated Romer, who could hardly help laughing to see the consternation depicted on some of the faces around them, at the profanity of his friend's answers.

"I didn't see any," was Captain Romilly's reply.

"What no young ladies fresh from England; nor fascinating widows on the look out for number two! I heard there had been quite an importation by the last steamer."

"I believe I was introduced to two or three girls just fresh from their boarding-schools; but they looked so horribly as if they expected me to propose to them, each time I opened my mouth, that I was afraid to cultivate their acquaintance. And as for the widows, Romer, you ought to know better than to mention them to a fellow just before dinner-time. Fact is," and here Captain Romilly drew out his cigar-case, and proceeded with a critical eye to select his next victim, "I haven't seen a woman, fit to be called a woman, since I came to this infernal country."

At this assertion, which rung like flat blasphemy in the ears of those who listened, a considerable commotion was apparent amongst the various members of the reading-room; and a little old man, dressed in a tight suit of native cloth, who had hardly been able to keep silence for some minutes past, sprung from his seat, and advancing to where Captain Romilly stood by the side of his friend, spluttered out :—

"If you say that, sir, you cannot boast the acquaintance of either Mrs. Colonel Dowdson, or Mrs. General MacSquirt, both of whom, I will venture to affirm, are as fine women as you will meet anywhere in the United Kingdom of Great Britain and Ireland!"

At this unwarrantable intrusion, Gordon Romilly gazed down on the incensed speaker, standing many inches below him, much as a mastiff might calmly contemplate an irritated cur—and was silent.

"Let me introduce you to General Perkins," said Captain Romer, hoping thereby to prevent anything unpleasant occurring from the interruption. Captain Romilly bowed, but still declined to speak.

"You cannot have seen either Mrs.

MacSquirt, or Mrs. Dowdson, sir," repeated the infuriated little General, throwing down the gauntlet a second time.

"I have not had that honour," replied Captain Romilly in his most throaty tones, as he bit off the end of his cigar, and turned it several times between his lips; and then addressing his friend, he continued, "Romer! don't you think we might have a weed together outside? I fancy this place is getting a little too hot for me."

Upon which the young men strolled out of the reading-room, and the club members threw down their books and papers, and entered into a noisy discussion concerning the individuality of the stranger.

"Who is he?" "What is his name?" "What does he belong to?" were the questions which eagerly poured from all sides; and an outcry was immediately raised for the club waiter to produce the book in which visitors wrote down their names and addresses upon first arrival.

"Captain the Honourable Gordon

Romilly, A.D.C.," was the last insertion there, and then a gentlemanly man with grey hair, who had kept silence hitherto, volunteered to furnish the desired information.

"I can tell you all about him," he said quietly, "for my friend Kinnaird is intimate with the family. He is the youngest son of Lord Erskine Romilly; grandson to the Earl of Bournemouth, and A.D.C. to the present Governor. He belongs to the Rifle Brigade, and took up his appointment in Madras, a few months ago, when young Plowden was invalided home. A fine young man! as far as personal appearance goes."

"A conceited puppy!" growled General Perkins, but the opinion no longer met with unqualified assent. Captain Gordon Romilly was conceited no doubt, and a puppy into the bargain, but he was the son of a Lord, and grandson to an Earl, and Honourables are too scarce in India, to be sniffed at with impunity.

Meanwhile Captain Romer had ordered his pony-phaeton to the door, and proposed to take the new comer a drive round the lake.

"I will point out some of our hill beauties to your notice, Romilly," he said as he gathered up the reins, and the spirited little animals he drove set off at a swinging trot down the steep decline, "and you shall see whether they do not contrast favourably with those you have left behind you in the plains."

"I hope you won't take the trouble to do any such thing," exclaimed the A.D.C. languidly, as he settled himself down amongst the cushions; "because if they're really pretty, I shall be getting an introduction to them; and I didn't come up to the hills with the intention of going through that kind of business."

"Are you afraid that love-making would prove too hard work for your delicate constitution," exclaimed Captain Romer, laughing.

"I really don't think anything about the matter. I'm happy to say I never experienced the sensation; and hope I never shall; for if what fellows tell me on the subject, is truth, it must be deucedly fatiguing."

"And yet you came here for a *change!*" said his friend, merrily.

CHAPTER II.

THE MISSIONARY'S FAMILY.

"But tell me truly, Romilly," continued Captain Romer more seriously, as the ponies landed them on level ground, and they commenced to make the circuit of the lake. "What is it, in this country, with which you find such fault?"

"With everything and everybody, my dear fellow," was the decided reply. "The climate is simply abominable, the people, for the most part, stuck-up, and intensely opinionated; and there is no earthly enjoyment, that I can see, to be extracted from any part of this quarter of the globe."

"With the first clause of your argument, I have no intention to combat," said

Romer, "there is no doubt that the climate is utterly unsuited to our English constitutions, and those men who are able to live in it, become so enervated and dried-up, and unlike their former selves, that they appear unfitted for any atmosphere but that which has ruined them. But I have received a great deal of hospitality and kindness from my countrymen in India; so that I do not like to hear you pass so sweeping a condemnation on them."

"I speak of a man as I find him," said Romilly carelessly, "and perhaps I have not happened to come across your friends. The people I have been introduced to, have been well enough as long as I praised Indian manners and customs; but once compare them unfavourably with those of England, and they were up in arms immediately."

"Well, it is natural, is it not? This is their adopted country; they are right to stand up for her."

"Very natural, doubtless, but uncommonly disagreeable at the same time. It riles a fellow to hear them talking of Madras institutions, and entertainments, and ceremonies, as though they were the grandest the world had ever produced. Why, would you believe, that one woman had the assurance to tell me, at a Government House dinner, that she supposed I had never seen so large a party assembled before?"

Captain Romilly put this last question so seriously, that he infinitely amused his friend.

"I can quite believe it, Romilly, and also that the lady was perfectly sincere in making the assertion."

"Well, then, she must have been a fool," rejoined the other, not over politely, "or could know nothing of the way in which we live in England."

"There you've hit it, Romilly! For the most part they do know nothing of what we call 'society' at home. They come out to India, fresh from their boarding-schools; and if they visit it at intervals, it is generally in the capacity of parents with large families, and when they are under the necessity of economising by hiding their heads in furnished apartments, or burying themselves, somewhere in the depths of the country. You can't expect them to have any knowledge of the method of living amongst the higher classes of England, for they have never seen it!"

"Then why do they brag so? They talk of their dances, and their dresses, and their suppers, as though they were the best in the world; and yet I have never been to a ball in India which could compare with a respectable one at home!"

"Because they are the best in the world to them," replied Romer, "Madras is their London, and Government House, their Buckingham Palace. We brag of ours, don't we?"

"Well! it's aggravating, to say the least of it," returned Captain Romilly. "They talk so big whilst they're in India, and when they go home, suddenly collapse and are nobody."

"To which lamentable conclusion, your displeasure may safely leave them, with every prospect of being amply revenged," said his friend. "I think there is no more pitiable sight than the spectacle of some old Colonel's or General's better half who has been lording it for years over the inferior officers and their wives, in India; landed in England, still bristling with the pride of importance, to find herself in twelve hours, just nowhere at all! No wonder the generality of them hate a country, where, if a woman has nothing in herself to recommend her, we have no time to take her husband's length of service into consideration; and where Generals' wives, and Subalterns' wives find alike, that without a certain income it is impossible to keep pace with the herd. In England, everyone finds his level: that soon takes their bragging out of them, poor things! and so, Romilly, I think we needn't grudge it to them whilst they are here."

"I'm sure I don't care what they do,"

replied the A.D.C., yawning, "so long as they don't ask me to listen to them. I am quit of it for sixty days, at all events, so let us be thankful for small mercies."

"Well, I'm not sure that I can promise you that the Ootacamundians shall be entirely free from the same weakness," said Captain Romer, laughing: "but you need not throw yourself in the way of it, unless you choose. What do you think of the cantonment from this point of view? You will, at least, acknowledge that we might boast of the scenery, without exaggeration."

"Exactly so, only you didn't make it. I admit that it is lovely. I have no fault to find with it, and could exclaim with the inspired Watts:

'That every prospect pleases, and only man is vile.'

Will you have a cigar?"

"Thanks! it wasn't Watts who wrote that line, by-the-bye, but the quotation is too apt to be quarrelled with. If you admire lovely scenery, we can shew you lots about here, Romilly. You have come in the very nick of time, for Newland is here at present, and we are going after ibex to-morrow morning, and shall be delighted with your company. You remember Newland, don't you?"

"I can't say I do."

"What, not Henry Newland? that very tall fellow, who used to be in the first form at the college? Perhaps not, though; he must have been near leaving when you arrived. He's up here now, however, and a crack shot. By the way, Romilly, he's a widower, his wife died a few months ago, and they say he was most awfully cut up about it, so don't talk of the happiness of married life, or anything of that sort before him."

"Am I likely?" pathetically demanded Captain Romilly. "I didn't even know there was such a thing."

"I'm afraid you're a bit of a misanthrope," said genial-hearted Romer; "but if so, you've come to the best place in which to be cured. There's nothing like a good stalk over these breezy hills to make a man feel in charity with his fellow creatures, and in a good temper with his dinner. We'll try the remedy on you tomorrow, Romilly, and you shall see that it will work like a charm."

"You quite mistake my disposition, my dear Romer," said Captain Romilly, "for I'm one of the easiest, best-tempered fellows going; but it is impossible for me to speak of what I know nothing. I never cared for a woman yet, and I never expect to care for one; therefore the pleasures to which you allude are as sealed books to me, either in experience or imagination. I have never had anything to do with the sex, from my royal mother downwards, but it ended in some trouble or other; so I've determined to keep my hands clear of them for the future."

"A very good determination," said Romer, "and one which the Neilgherry Hills are not likely to afford you much temptation to break. If you will join our shooting party, Romilly, I promise you

you shall encounter no more dangerous ladies than the poor does, and you are more likely to break their hearts, than they are to break yours."

"It would take a great many ladies to do that," remarked the A.D.C., sententiously.

'They had just arrived at the end of the lake, where a curve in the road would put the ponies' heads in a homeward direction, along the opposite side, and from which several paths, branching over the hills, led to various scattered houses, a little distance from the cantonment.

"We will turn here," observed Captain Romilly, "and we shall reach the hotel just as dinner is being placed on the table."

But at that moment, as he commenced to walk the ponies round the curve alluded to, the figure of a woman, who, with a wild and hurried air was muttering to herself, as she went, walked rapidly past them. Her manner was so extraordinary, and the few words which dropped from her lips as she passed so incoherent, that she attracted the attention of both the young men, and they looked at one another in surprise.

"What *can* be the matter?" whispered Captain Romer to his friend.

"Mad!" suggested Gordon Romilly, "or drunk, perhaps."

"No! no! nothing of the kind," was the prompt reply, "why, it's Mrs. Ward, the missionary's wife. Hold the ribbons a moment, Romilly; I must speak to her," and without waiting for assent, he threw the reins to his companion, and jumping out of the phaeton, ran after the striding figure.

"Mrs. Ward! is anything the matter? can I do anything for you?"

At the sound of his friendly voice, the woman stopped and looked him vacantly in the face. She was a thin, middle-aged creature, with a worn and patient countenance, whose cotton dress and washed-out shawl clung painfully round her attenuated form, revealing but too certainly the want of under garments; but the most pitiful things about her were her eyes, which looked as though she were walking in her sleep, and unable to comprehend what passed around her.

"Mrs. Ward!" repeated Captain Romer, alarmed at her appearance, "are you not well?—will you let me take you home?"

"I'm all right, thank you!" she said in a hurried, nervous manner. "They say that there's been an accident, and some one's killed; and they fetched me from the town, where I had gone to—dear me! where did I leave my basket?" she continued wanderingly, as she turned her head in all directions, and then, re-fixing her gaze upon Captain Romer—"there's been an accident, no doubt, and some one's killed; but it cannot be my Alice, it cannot possibly be my Alice."

"If there has been an accident at home, and you are going there," exclaimed Captain Romer, "let me drive you, Mrs. Ward! You cannot walk so fast as I can take you in the pony-chaise. Come! let us go at once."

He dragged her hastily towards the

phaeton: and almost lifted her up into the seat.

"Romilly, my dear fellow! You won't mind taking the back seat for ten minutes, will you? Some report has reached Mrs. Ward—exaggerated no doubt—of an accident having taken place at her home, and she is anxious to reach it as soon as possible. Keep up your courage, Mrs. Ward, my ponies are stout little fellows, and will take us over the hill in no time. I daresay after all, it will prove a false alarm."

But Mrs. Ward was in no condition to listen to any of his kind assurances. Relieved from the temporary pressure that excitement had put upon her, the poor creature had leisure to realise the horrors she was anticipating, and with a half-smothered exclamation of "it can't be my Alice!" sunk down almost insensible at the bottom of the pony-chaise.

"What is it?" whispered Romilly in his friend's ear.

"I can hardly say: I think she has heard bad news. Poor thing! she is the very best of creatures. We must get her home as soon as possible," and, whipping his animals into a gallop, Captain Romer sent his phaeton, bounding and jolting in the most unorthodox manner, over the stony road which led to the missionary's house. A few minutes' drive took them to the top of the hill, on the other side of which, lying in a hollow, they could see Mrs. Ward's home. The descent to it was too steep for the phaeton to traverse, even had it not been only an irregular path strewn with sharp flints; and as Captain Romer drew rein, and the panting ponies obeyed the motion of his hand, he could see that the plot of grass in front of the building was covered with quite a crowd of natives.

"I'm really afraid there has been an accident," he remarked to Captain Romilly as he stood up to survey the scene; "what shall we do next?"

"Oh, let me go! let me go!" cried Mrs. Ward, as she struggled into a sitting position; and Romilly had just sprung out to assist her to the ground, when a grey-haired man toiled up the rocky path to meet them.

"Emma, it was the will of God!" he said in a solemn tone as he took hold of his wife's hand.

"Not Alice, George! not Alice!" she shrieked, looking wildly in his face.

"Yes, Alice. Has He not the right to take which He chooses?"

But the poor mother was unable to reason or to reply. She sank down again insensible where she stood, and Captain Romer assisted her husband to carry her into the house—where Romilly, after having procured a native to hold the ponies' heads, was too interested not to follow them. As he reached the lawn in front of it, the little crowd separated, and disclosed a sight so startling to his eyes, that he sickened and turned pale. On its back, extended on the grass, was lying the corpse of a fine girl of about fourteen or fifteen years old, but who looked, as is usual with English children reared upon the Neilgherries, much older. Her fair unbound hair was streaming on the grass beside her; her stockingless feet and legs, barely covered sufficiently for decency by her scanty petticoats, were marble in their whiteness, and her blue eyes, unclosed, were staring upwards to the sky, as though appealing to Heaven against the cruel death which had so suddenly snapped the thread of her young life. Every now and then, an inquisitive native would attempt to raise the corpse; and Romilly could see, by the way the head fell back, that the unfortunate girl had broken her neck. Feeling almost unable to endure so sad a sight, he shudderingly turned aside in search of his friend Romer, and encountered him on his way back to join him.

"What a horrible accident!" he ejaculated.

"Horrible indeed! it seems the poor child, in company with her brothers and sisters, was amusing herself by riding a half-trained pony up and down that rocky path. It had on a boy's saddle with an iron stirrup, in which her foot somehow got twisted, and before she could disengage herself, the brute threw her, and then dragged her down the hill, striking her head on the stones at every step. When he landed her on the lawn, the father says she was quite dead? There is an awful scene going on in there; and, to tell you the truth, Romilly, I don't feel as though I could stand it much longer, and as we can't be of any further use, I think we had better go home."

"But is *that* to lie out here all night," said Captain Romilly, pointing to the body of the dead girl, "to be pulled about by these curious natives? Surely they ought to carry it into the house!"

"I should think so; but there seems no woman here to take the direction of things, and I hardly like to interfere. The poor mother is utterly incapable, and the father seems little better. I never saw people so utterly prostrated by a blow as they appear to be by this. And yet they have nine children left, and scarcely bread to give them. One would have thought they could have spared a daughter!"

"She seems to have been a fine girl," said Captain Romilly.

"Yes. Poor little Alice! How often I have seen her running about the cantonment!"

"I don't half like to go and leave her lying out here," said his friend musingly.

But whilst they deliberated on their best course of action, a commotion was visible amongst the assemblage of natives, who first spoke a few words to one another and then drew back as though to make way for some one; but before Romer and Romilly had time to speculate on the new arrival, a rich, pathetic voice, exclaiming—

"*Ah! ma petite! est-ce vraiment toi?*" sounded on the air; and a young girl rushed suddenly between them and the dead body of Alice Ward, and threw herself upon the grass beside it.

"*Est-ce vraiment toi? Ah! mon Dieu, ayez pitié de nous.*"

She lifted up the dead face, tenderly put

away the stray locks of hair which had fallen over it, pressed it eagerly to her own, and feeling its unnatural coldness, burst into a flood of tears.

Meanwhile, the two friends could only gaze at her in silent surprise. No taller and much slighter than the body she embraced, it was yet evident from the maturity of her figure, that she was several years older than Alice Ward had been, although the long black cloak which she wore, only allowed her shape to be revealed by glimpses. She had no covering on her head, and her dark hair was bound closely to it by two long, thick plaits which fell below her waist. In her ears she wore a pair of large gold earrings, very old-fashioned and curious in appearance, and yet her shapely feet were but indifferently covered, and the rest of her costume betokened poverty. Her burst of grief was transitory as it was sudden; in another moment she had turned a pair of dark blue eyes, glittering with emotion, upon them and saying rapidly—

"*Pardon ! mais c'est bien triste, n'est-ce pas ?*" rose to her feet and brushed her tears hastily away. "*Il ne faut pas qu'elle reste ici,*" she resumed, appealing to Captain Romer; and then perceiving the look of incomprehension on the face of her listener, she repeated rather slowly, and with a slight French accent—"She must not rest here, gentlemen; aid me to carry her to her bed."

She unbuttoned her cloak at the throat as she spoke, and threw it over the body, revealing white arms bare to above the elbows, and a fair throat and neck, over which a little red neckerchief was quaintly crossed and pinned. Then she stooped, placing her hands beneath the shoulders of the corpse, and Captain Romer and his friend gently raising the lower part of the body they carried it together through the passage of the house, up the narrow stairs to the scantily-furnished bedroom, and placed it reverently on the bed, whence it had risen that morning in life and health. As soon as it was disposed there, the girl, heedless apparently of the presence of the two men, drew a silver crucifix from her bosom, kissed, and placed it on that of the corpse, and sank down upon her knees in prayer. They lingered for a moment to watch her clasped hands and uplifted eyes, and would then have turned away and left her to herself, but that she rose from her position, and with a slight serious inclination of the head, ran past them down the stairs, whilst they picked their way after her, fearful of disturbing the bereaved parents in the room below. They could hear the moaning of the poor mother as they passed it, and the foreign accents of the young stranger speaking some words of consolation, and the father met them at the door with a few broken sentences of gratitude for all that they had done, which they were thankful to escape.

As they again stepped out upon the grass plat, the moon had risen, the band of natives had dispersed, and everything looked calm and peaceful. Their pony phaeton was in waiting for them at the top of the hill, and as they found themselves on the road to the cantonment again, they simultaneously gave vent to their feelings in a long sigh of relief.

"I shall never care to drive round that way again," said Captain Romer, "I don't know when I've witnessed anything that made me feel so queer as I have done to-night."

"I can quite understand it," replied Gordon Romilly. "I never wish to see such another sight. But I say, Romer—I wonder who the deuce that little girl with the long hair is. She was the only one who seemed to have her wits about her."

"I've not the slightest notion! The thought of the poor parents' grief haunts me so, that I had almost forgotten her. No relation evidently, because she is a Roman Catholic. There are lots of them about here! Good heavens! that there should be such misery in the world. No need to warn one against talking too much of the happiness of married life after this; eh, Romilly?"

"I never did talk of it, did I?" returned the A.D.C. in his most sententious tone.

CHAPTER III.

THE AVALANCHE BUNGALOW.

The next morning was bright and cloudless; and as the young men met at the door of the club, preparatory to starting on their shooting excursion, they felt that much of the painful impression received the day before, had been dispelled by a good night's rest.

Romer, and Major Newland, were mounted on stout hill ponies; but Gordon Romilly rode a high-mettled Arab, which, much against the advice of his friends, he had insisted upon taking up to the Neilgherries with him. As he bestrode it, with the half-careless, half-insolent air which became his handsome face so well, he formed so fine a picture, that even the worst enemies he had made on the previous day, could not but acknowledge that the Governor's aide-de-camp was uncommonly good-looking; and Colonel Greene, the gentleman who had recorded his pedigree for the benefit of the club members, went up and spoke to him, introducing himself through the name of his friend Kinnaird.

At which mention, Captain Romilly shewed there were two sides to his character, for his face lit up with genuine friendliness, and his grasp of Colonel Greene's proffered hand was hearty and sincere.

"Kinnaird! the very best fellow going; I am proud to meet one of his friends. And so you know something of my family, sir! Sorry to hear it, for taking one with another, I'm afraid they're a very bad lot! Have you seen Kinnaird lately?"

"Not since last year; for he is holding an appointment in the Punjaub. I hope your father, and the rest of the family are well?"

"My father is not well, thank you; he

has been a martyr to the gout for the last six months."

"Nothing alarming, I trust?"

"Oh! by no means; not half alarming enough in fact, or he might be induced to allow me to return to England, instead of insisting upon my remaining in this detestable country until the Governor dispenses with my services. It'll be the death of me, I'm convinced of that. However, I'm only a younger son, so I suppose it won't much signify."

"I'll think you'll survive it a little longer," said Colonel Greene smiling.

"That's all you know about it, sir. You judge by my exterior, like most other people. You don't know what I have to suffer internally, every day of my life."

"I know one thing, my young friend," said the old man, as he approached nearer to Gordon Romilly, and laid his hand upon his saddle-bow. "I see that you're inclined to be a little bit discontented, and to view all things here in their worst light. But take the advice of an old soldier, and treat India, (whilst you are in it) as we are cautioned to treat our wives—

> 'Be to her faults a little blind;
> And to her virtues, very kind.'

It's the only way to get on out here!"

"But I don't want to get on," replied Gordon Romilly, half-smiling and half-serious, "my only desire is to get off."

"You're incorrigible!" laughed Colonel Greene; and the order to start being given, with a few words of farewell, the shooting party rode out of the *compound*.

"When did our baggage go on?" demanded Captain Romilly, as they rode abreast through the cantonment roads.

"This morning at five o'clock," replied Romer, "I was virtuous enough to rise, and see it all dispatched myself. We have nine women coolies and two bullocks."

"Nine women, and two bullocks! In the name of Heaven, how long do you intend to stay in the wilderness?"

"Five or six days, if it suits us," replied Captain Romer; "but remember, Romilly, we have to provide food for all the servants who accompany us, as well as carry 'gram' for the horses. I can assure you we shall not live luxuriously, for I have only been able to send on the merest necessaries for ourselves."

"Who needs or expects to live luxuriously when out shooting?" remarked Major Newland, a tall, gaunt, taciturn man. "A true sportsman cares for nothing so long as he has enough to eat."

"Oh! of course, of course," said Gordon Romilly, who was very apt to agree with what his friends said, to save himself the trouble of argument. In reality however he was much too selfish, and too sensuously-inclined to make a keen sportsman, although his self-esteem prevented him from acknowledging the fact.

"How far shall we go this afternoon?" he demanded presently of Captain Romer.

"To the Avalanche Bungalow, where we shall dine and sleep. It is only distant eleven miles, but as soon as we are clear of the cantonment we shall have to travel very slowly, for it is all up and down hill, and in places very slippery. Have an eye to that horse of yours, Romilly! He'll have you over the precipice if you allow him to dance about in that absurd manner."

Captain Romer's prophecy being literally in danger of fulfilment, it was some little while before the Arab's master could put the question he had been about to ask, of why the Avalanche Bungalow had been so named.

"I really can't tell you for certain," replied Romer; " but some people say that an avalanche of earth fell near the spot years ago, so I suppose that is the reason."

"It sounds so devilishly romantic," resumed Romilly, "that I expect to see a Hebe in short petticoats and thick ankles, tripping down the steps of a vine-covered *châlet* to receive us as we arrive."

At this instance of the A.D.C.'s frivolity, Major Newland gave a grunt of dissatisfaction.

"You'll find it 'devilishly romantic,' if your horse takes you over the side," he said, observing that the antics of Romilly's steed had not yet subsided; whilst Captain Romer begged him not to raise his hopes as high as his horse's heels.

"The bungalow itself is picturesque enough," he said, "but instead of a Hebe to wait on you, Romilly, you'll have to put up with the attendance of an old withered native man, in a pair of cloth trousers, and a linen 'puggry.'"

At which prospect Captain Romilly made a wry face, and said it was just what he might have expected in such an abominable and heathenish country.

But when at five o'clock in the afternoon they came in sight of the Avalanche Bungalow, even Captain Romilly's spleen was powerless to prevent his expressing his admiration at the sight. At the foot of a high hill, the lower part of which was thickly covered with vegetation, stood a small building, formed of wood, and having something the appearance of a Swiss cottage, which was entirely shut in on three sides by the surrounding jungle, and in front of which ran a stream of the purest water. The appearance of this little shooting box, all ready to receive them, seemed to put fresh vigour into the travellers, who were wearied, not so much by the distance they had come, as by the slow progress they had been forced to make, and they gladly pressed forward to the door. Their servants having arrived before them, their dinner was prepared, and ready to be placed on the table, as soon as they should have refreshed themselves after their ride; but Major Newland's native servant, who had been appointed *major domo* of the commissariat department, met them at the door with a long face, as he informed them that the cow belonging to the man in charge of the bungalow had been carried off by a tiger the night before; and therefore he had been unable to procure any milk for their coffee.

"A tiger!" exclaimed Major Newland, his dull face brightening up as nothing yet had enabled it to do; "and only last night. Here's luck!" and calling to his "shikarry," he commenced a rapid conversation with him in Hindustani, during which it would have been hard to say whether the master or the servant gesticulated most.

"No milk!" said Captain Romer, "well, Daniel, I suppose there's a cocoa-nut to be got about here, anyhow."

"What will be the use of that?" demanded Romilly, as he jumped off his horse, which had fretted itself into a perfect lather from the unusual restraint which had been placed upon its actions. "You're not going to put any of that nasty stuff they call milk into our coffee, I hope, for I shall prefer *café noir.*"

"No! but Daniel will express some milk from the nut itself, you ignoramus; and if I hadn't said anything about it, I daresay you would never have found out the difference."

As soon as Major Newland could be persuaded to leave off calculating his chances of tracking the marauding tiger of the night before, and to betake himself to his dressing-room, the friends separated to make a hasty toilette before the dinner was served up; but Captain Romilly had hardly plunged his head and face into cold water, before Romer burst into his presence again, brimful of a fresh piece of news, which he delivered in his usual hearty manner.

"I say Romilly, old fellow, by the living jingo, here's the greatest bit of good luck that ever befell a man. Just fancy! here's Powell located in this very bungalow, and he says if we'll go out with him to-morrow, that he'll shew us no end of ibex, and—"

"And who the devil is Powell?" said Romilly, lifting his head out of the basin, and looking like the rose of a watering-pot.

"Powell! why he's the best fellow possible to go about with out here; he knows every inch of this part of the hills, and has shot over it scores of times. I've asked him to join his dinner to ours, (that's a common thing when chums meet together at these out-of-the-way places, you know), and it'll all be ready in another minute. Make haste with your dressing!"

4—2

"How can you expect a man to make haste, whilst you require an answer to your remarks every second? Go away, do, Romer, and then I may have a chance of getting some dinner before that long fellow, Newland, swallows it, table and all."

Upon which Captain Romer disappeared, laughing and whistling, and for the next ten minutes the conversation with his friend Powell, carried on from the dressing-room to the general sitting-room, was the only sound to be heard in the bungalow.

When the four men met at the dinner-table, they promised to make a very agreeable party. Major Powell proved to be a regular old Indian, with thin grey hair, a rough weather-tanned complexion, and a keen sportsman-like eye. He welcomed Major Newland and Captain Romilly, as if he had known them for years; congratulated them on the treat in store for them, if luck attended their sport, and affirmed that though he had stalked in the Highlands, shot in the Himalayas, and even hunted on the prairies of South America, he had never had better sport than he had enjoyed on the Neilgherry Hills.

"We are most anxious to get some ibex," observed Captain Romer, as they settled themselves at table. "Newland, who has slain his tigers by the dozen, has not accomplished an ibex yet, and I have never even tried for one."

"They are very difficult game, as perhaps you are aware, and require more patience in stalking than any other species; not only on account of their long scent, which is marvellously fine, but their instinct, which never permits a buck to feed without a sentinel beside him to warn him of approaching danger."

"How very curious!" observed Captain Romilly.

"It is true nevertheless, and for this reason, although they usually feed on the heights, leaving the does and young in the valleys, and are visible in this clear air from a great distance, it is extremely difficult to approach them without being perceived. However I have no doubt that you gentlemen have plenty of patience, and plenty of courage, and with it, every prospect of success; and I shall be delighted if my hints can be of any use to you. Have you had any experience of shooting in this country?" addressing himself to Romilly.

"None whatever, I have only been out here three months, and this is my first visit to the hills."

"Then you are about to see India under her most favourable aspect," said Major Powell with a grim expression. "There is nothing in the place worth living for, except the shooting."

"Now, Romilly!" cried Romer gaily, "you and Powell can have a good dish of abuse together against the country. I don't think you can hate it more than he does; he has always been an inveterate grumbler."

"Do you dislike it?" asked Romilly, quickly turning to Major Powell.

"Mortally," was the decided reply, "and I have good reason to do so. It has killed half my relations, and sent the other half to the dogs. I hate everything connected with it, except the sport."

"Then, why do you stay here?"

"For the best of reasons; because I can't help myself. I don't suppose any man, with a soul, would do otherwise. The country is all very well for those it was made for, but it's not a fit place for Christians."

"Particularly when their literary productions are not appreciated by the public press," laughed Romer.

"Oh! I've got over that old sore long ago," replied Major Powell.

"May I ask to what you allude?" said Romilly.

"Certainly, it is no secret. Some years back, I was fool enough to imagine that I had discovered a means by which I might benefit my fellow creatures, by rendering the method of instruction in drill less monotonous and less puzzling than it is at present. I worked for a long time at my manual until I had brought it to perfection;

and several superior officers who took the trouble to listen to my explanations, considering the plan would be a successful one, I went to the expense of having my rules and diagrams printed; confidently expecting to receive, at least, a few thanks for my pains."

"It is not often that Government repays her benefactors in any heavier coin," remarked Romilly. "But what was the issue?"

"The issue, my dear fellow, was—smoke! Still, I never will believe but that my pamphlet would have attracted notice from head quarters, had it not been so roughly handled by the local papers."

"But what was their object?"

"None! excepting to annoy me. But, having unfortunately alluded, in a sort of preface which I wrote to the work, to the dormant state of the native faculties, and the necessity there was for presenting everything to their imaginations, in the simplest guise, I suppose I hit some of the sub-editors or writers, rather hard, and they revenged themselves in consequence, by damning my manual."

"How could such an allusion affect them?" demanded Romilly.

"My dear Romilly, don't you know that most of these fellows who have anything to do with the local Indian papers, are half castes," said Captain Romer, "and of course they don't like the dormant state of the faculties of their nearest relations alluded to in that cool manner. How would you like the dormant state of the faculties of your mama or papa, shown up in public print? It was cruel of Powell, as I've always told him, and he ought to have had more consideration for their feelings."

Major Powell shrugged his shoulders and laughed. "Well, it's all over now, and the less said about it the better, but I've made my last attempt to improve the condition of my fellow creatures. They may march out of step, and get themselves into inextricable confusion on the brigade grounds to all eternity, before I'll ever attempt to make the business plainer to their dormant faculties again. I've done with philanthropising, or being a 'man and a brother' either."

"But excuse me if I say," observed Captain Romilly, "that it seems incredible to me how anyone could mind attacks from such quarters, any more than you would heed the snapping of a mongrel cur. Why, I should have thought that a glance at one of their local papers, was sufficient to decide the worth of their criticisms. Printed on tea-paper, with every other word spelled wrong, and the rules of grammar 'nowhere;' how is it possible that their reviews can affect the success of any book? Even were they universally read and believed, they can only bias the opinion of residents in India, and what are they, compared to the mass of minds to be swayed in England? A drop of water to the ocean."

"True, my dear Romilly, all perfectly true: but when the cur is determined to bite, he can draw blood as well as a nobler animal, and it is a well known fact that government throws every obstacle she can in the path of her inventive offspring; on the principle, I suppose, of the North American Indians, who half-murder their children in order to find out which are the strongest and best able to survive the treatment."

"Have done!" cried Romer emphatically, as having finished their meal, the four men rose from table, and ensconced themselves comfortably before the little wood fire which their servants had kindled : " I vote that Government, the Indian press, and her majesty's British possessions in the east, are from this moment subjects utterly tabooed, and that Powell gives us his last hunting adventure as a change. Come, Powell! you owe us something in return for the patience with which poor Newland here, and myself, have been listening to your abuse of our adored adopted country."

"My last hunting adventure," replied Major Powell, as he lit a huge meerschaum, and commenced, in company with his friends, to fill the room with smoke, "dates no further back than yesterday morning, but I daresay it will be not the less acceptable to you for being new. I was strolling out with my gun after nothing particular, when I came upon two tigers hunting samber on their own account: and as I was too far off to get a shot at them, I just sat down quietly to watch the sport, thinking that when the tigers were busy with their prey, I might have an opportunity of spoiling their little game. I saw one of the brutes conceal himself in a narrow gorge, which he evidently expected the deer would pass; whilst the other made a *détour* so as to get beyond the herd, and drive it towards the hiding-place of his companion."

"What cunning," observed Major Newland.

"Oh! the instinct of these animals is marvellous: I could tell you a dozen stories much more wonderful than this, only Romer asked for the very last. Well, the tiger having succeeded in creeping round the herd, advanced cautiously upon them: but the samber were too quick for him, and bolted before he was near enough to spring; and his friend in the gorge was likewise disappointed, for the herd passed far beyond his reach. I then thought it was time for me to appear upon the scene of action, but before I could get within shot of them, the two tigers walked off together into a sholah where it would have been foolhardiness in me to follow them. I never was more put out in my life. But, talking of tigers, did I never tell you of my friend Blast, who succeeded in getting three at one time to his own gun, in the Annomally Forests?"

"Three tigers all at once! Powell, you must be joking."

"I'm in sober earnest, Romer, and you will allow they must have made a very pretty bag. I forget the exact circumstances of the case, as it happened many years ago; but I know that as he was walking with a native attendant looking after some of the government timber which was in his charge, he suddenly came upon three tigers who had just gorged themselves on the carcase of a samba, and were lying under a tree fast asleep. Blast shot two of them as they lay, right and left, and following up the third for a short distance, put a couple more bullets into him, and finished the business. I know this to be a fact, for my friend was anything but a boaster, and I have heard the story, and seen the three tiger skins, not once but a dozen times."

"Three tigers at a go!" exclaimed Romer, "well, that beats anything I ever heard. Come, Romilly, if you've any idea of emulating that feat, I think it's time we turned in, and took a little rest beforehand," and with many good wishes for the next day's sport, the friends separated for the night.

CHAPTER IV.

LOST AMONG THE PRECIPICES.

At an early hour the next morning, the sportsmen were again astir, and it was agreed over the breakfast table that they should hunt in couples, and that as Romer and Romilly were strangers to the hills, the former should be the companion of Major Newland, and the latter, that of Major Powell, for the day.

"You have got the best of the bargain," said Romer, addressing himself to the aide-de-camp, "for I'd lay a poney, that if any game worth having is shot to-day, it will fall to Powell's gun. He is the luckiest beggar going—in that way."

"Ah! you may well add, 'in that way,' Master Romer," said the Major, laughing, "for it's the only way it has come to me yet."

"Now, not a word about the local papers 'an' thou lov'st me, Hal,'" said Romer, imploringly.

"I had no intention of alluding to them, you saucy younker! but I've no time to argue the subject with you to-day. I don't know what you two gentlemen intend to do, but Captain Romilly and I are going to ride out five miles towards 'Buffaloes' Swamp,' and then send our horses back by the horse-keepers."

"Perhaps we had better do the same in the opposite direction," said Major Newland; "it's no good tiring ourselves without cause."

"Certainly not; you will have had plenty of walking before we meet again; and so, Romilly, if you are ready we'll start at once. Good bye, Romer, good luck to you, and don't think of shewing your face here again without being able to produce a good fat ibex into the bargain!"

"In which case, say farewell to it for

ever!" quoth Romer pathetically; and then the first detachment of the shooting party rode away from the Avalanche Bungalow.

They had not gone many miles before they met a solitary native woman, walking so fast that she might almost be said to have been running, and evidently anxious to escape observation. She was very lightly clothed, and appeared so unfit to be travelling about the hills alone, that Major Powell sent his horsekeeper after her to ask where she had come from and where she was going to. At first she seemed very unwilling to give any information respecting herself; but on being pressed, confessed that she was journeying to Ootacamund, but still declined to say from what place she had started. Major Powell instructed his servant to try and persuade her to stay at the Avalanche Bungalow for the night, where he promised she should have food, and be allowed to go on the first thing in the morning; but the woman refused all his overtures of assistance with a hurried and frightened air, and seemed only anxious to be permitted to continue her journey undisturbed. When she had passed on, and Major Powell's horsekeeper had related the circumstances to his master, Captain Romilly asked him what interest he had in trying to stop the woman's progress.

"Simply in the cause of humanity," he answered. "It is impossible she can reach Ootacamund on foot before night, and she will probably lie down and die as soon as the darkness falls. These natives cannot stand the cold night air of the hills, especially with such inadequate clothing. But my horsekeeper tells me that she has run away from one of the coffee plantations hereabouts, before she has worked out the advance pay she has received; and she was afraid lest we should detain her, poor creature, and send her back again."

"A fugitive slave," exclaimed Romilly.

"Exactly so—and very likely from a master not much kinder than 'Legree.' But you can have no idea what numbers of coolies die on the hills during the rains from wet and cold. A man I know, not long ago found nine coolies sitting by the roadside in a pouring shower, who had evidently given in, and made up their minds to die. He gave them all the brandy which was in his flask; tried to persuade them to move on by every means in his power—even took to thrashing them to *force* them to exert themselves; but it was all of no avail. He was obliged at last to relinquish his benevolent intentions, for fear of being benighted himself; and the nine coolies were subsequently found dead."

"How incredible! and after their friend had taken the trouble to thrash them! Pure ingratitude I call it!"

"Ah! you may laugh, but it was the kindest thing he could have done for them. It shews how doggedly determined they must have been to commit suicide, not to have benefited by the hint. But only the other day a friend of mine going to see a beautiful view from a high hill not far from Ootacamund, found on its summit a dead native, who was proved on enquiry to have lost his way, been benighted, and died of cold. An European under such circumstances would have had the sense to keep moving about, but a native has no energy, he succumbs to his fate at once—like the Chinese, who are so used to be carried off by tigers that when they see one coming they quietly sit down, to save him the trouble of pursuing them any further."

"But I should think it was no joke to be lost upon these hills."

"No joke at all; the walking, in parts, is dangerous enough even by daylight; and at night each footstep becomes a fresh peril. But we must dismount here, Romilly, and send our horses back to the bungalow; our 'shikarries' and our guns are all we shall want for the remainder of the day."

Having dismissed their animals under the charge of their grooms, the two men first took their luncheon, and then, followed by their game-beaters, or "shikarries," toiled up and down some very steep hills for the best part of an hour, after which they sat down on the top of one of the highest, not only to take breath, but to survey the surrounding landscape, for which purpose Major Powell produced a powerful telescope. Having swept the horizon with it for a few minutes in silence, he handed it to his companion.

"Look in that direction, Romilly, towards the highest point beyond those two, and you will see something on the move, which, if I mistake not, are a couple of ibex."

"I see them," exclaimed Romilly, "I can see them plainly; but they must be nearly a mile distant. One is feeding, whilst the other stands perfectly motionless on a rock. Let's be after them at once!" and throwing down the telescope, in another second he was on his feet, and replacing the shot-belt and powder-flask which he had loosened from his shoulders.

"Gently, gently!" said Major Powell, amused at the other's eagerness: "if you go to work in this manner, my dear fellow, you will have the ibex a couple of miles the other way before you have had time to collect all your belongings."

"But it is impossible they can see us at this distance : we can only just make them out, even with the telescope."

"And they have a telescope in either eye ; and a scent so fine, that the air tells them of our approach long before we are in sight. If you want to get anywhere within range of them, you must follow my example."

Whereupon Major Powell commenced to creep in the direction of the ibex, climbing the acclivities on all fours, and cautiously examining each spot before he put down his foot on it, so that their progress was exceedingly tedious ; and Gordon Romilly, who had none of the old sportsman's patient deliberation, soon tired of the pursuit, and wanted to know, in a very audible whisper, whether they couldn't get on a little faster.

" Hush !" said Major Powell, emphasising the caution with knitted brows ; " you mustn't utter a syllable, Romilly, or you'll spoil sport. Look there ! the sentry evidently thinks that all is safe, for he has actually commenced to browse near his companion. We must make a wide circuit, to avoid giving them our wind, and perhaps we may be fortunate enough to get near to them."

They proceeded as before, with caution, which appeared to Captain Romilly very unnecessary, until they had advanced to within sixty yards of the game, still unperceived, when a thoughtless exclamation from the aide-de-camp startled the sentinel ibex, and both the animals darted off as hard as they could go.

Major Powell fired first at one, and then at the other, but, as they went on, apparently unhurt, he concluded that he must have missed them.

"You lost me that buck, Romilly," he said, almost testily, to his companion. "What the deuce you meant by holloaing out in that way, when I had just warned you to be quiet, I can't imagine! We shan't get within shot of anything if you are not more cautious—you can have no idea how sound is carried in this rarefied air—it's of no use our going on unless you can promise to be silent."

But here Captain Romilly apologised so

amply, that the Major was feign to be pacified.

"I'm awfully sorry, Powell; I am, indeed: but I touched up my favourite corn on a sharp piece of rock, and it isn't easy to hold one's tongue entirely under such circumstances."

"Don't say anything more about it, my dear fellow; I should have remembered that you're new to this sort of work. Now I wonder where the plague those two brutes have hid themselves. I'm sure I put a bullet into one, if not into both of them; and I think it will be worth our while to follow them up a bit."

The "shikarries," on being appealed to, said that the deer had run down a very steep hill before them, into a sholah; but they were both quite certain that neither of them had been hit by the Major Sahib's gun.

"They may be as sure as they like," remarked their employer to Captain Romilly, "but I happen to have an opinion of my own upon the subject; so with your leave,

Romilly, we'll make our way towards the sholah."

They began to descend the hill as he spoke, and had not gone many yards before they saw one of the ibex emerge from the other side of the brushwood, walking very slowly, and evidently wounded.

"That fellow's hit!" exclaimed Major Powell, his tanned face beaming with excitement, "and why is the other not with him? He would never have remained behind unless he were dead or badly wounded. Follow up the track at once," he continued, directing the "shikarries" in their native tongue, "and see if you cannot find him."

Almost as excited as their master by the sight of the wounded deer, the men now willingly set off in search of his companion, and before they had penetrated the sholah for more than a dozen yards, Powell and Romilly heard them calling out that they were successful.

"Come on, Romilly," cried the Major, as (regardless of thorns and briars) he prepared to plunge into the densely-wooded thicket, "here's an omen of good luck—we shall have the laugh over Newland and Romer yet!" and hurrying to the spot, they found the ibex lying dead on its back, amongst the bushes; and from its position, they perceived that it must have run to the edge of the sholah, and turned a somersault in dying. The difficulty now was how to get the animal out of the thicket, in order to skin it, for it was a very large and heavy male, and the sportsmen found that with the assistance of their "shikarries," they could not even lift it from the ground.

"I'll tell you what we must do, Romilly," said the Major, "we must all set to work with our hunting-knives, and cut away the branches, until we have made a path wide enough, through which to drag the brute, along to a more open spot. I shouldn't like to lose it, for although I have often killed ibex, I never brought down such a fine one before."

They all fell to work, and followed his advice, but it took them a long time to accomplish, and before they had skinned the ibex, and cut off its head for preservation, it was nearly dark.

"Good God! I had no idea it was so late as this!" exclaimed Major Powell, as he lifted up his heated face, streaming with the exertion he had undergone, and surveyed the fast increasing gloom; "what can we have been about to let the time pass so? Romilly! we mustn't loiter here another moment! Neither I nor my 'shikarries' are familiar with this particular part of the hills, and if we wait till the night has fallen we may experience some difficulty in finding our way; that's the worst of the Neilgherries, there is no twilight here, and if you are not continually consulting your watch, you have the place pitch-dark before you know where you are."

Captain Romilly and himself took the charge of their own guns as he spoke, and the head and skin of the ibex being carried by the "shikarries," the party commenced as quickly as they could, to reascend the steep, rocky hill before them. But the gentlemen found the rapid and irregular climbing so unusual an exertion, and the weight of their weapons added so much to their fatigue, that Romilly soon proposed that the ibex skin and head should be left behind them till the morning, when the "shikarries" might return and fetch them.

"They would be devoured, or at least spoiled by jackals in the night," returned Major Powell, "so if we wish to preserve a trophy of our adventure, Romilly, we must struggle on a little longer as we are."

They toiled on again, jumping over ditches, pushing their way through bushes, and almost tumbling on their noses at every other step they took.

"Are you sure we are in the right track?" said Romilly, panting, "I don't remember coming across all these bushes in our descent?"

"Don't question it, man, for Heaven's sake," was Major Powell's reply, "only mind your footing, and push on as fast as you can, till we have left these treacherous hills behind us."

By this time the evening had grown so dark that they could not see their hands before them, and Powell could hear the natives behind him grumbling at the turn affairs had taken, and telling one another that they had not the least idea where they were going. The walking, which was bad enough in the day time, had now become quite dangerous; every moment the sportsmen hit their feet against large stones or pieces of loose rock, which bounded from beneath their tread, and fell down unknown depths, where they almost feared that they should follow them, and the "shikarries'" constant warning cry of "precipice," sounded terrible in the darkness.

Major Powell was growing very anxious, but he did not like to communicate his fears to his companion, lest he should unnecessarily depress his spirits, but kept up a continual jesting instead, on the evil adventure which had befallen them, whilst Romilly followed closely on his heels, not nervous, though rather silent, and only occasionally startled by the earnestness of his friend's caution that he should be careful where he trod.

At last, however, the "shikarries," having collected sufficient dry wood as they walked, lighted a small fire, from which each of the four men selected the largest brands to serve for torches, and by the light they afforded them, fancying they were not quite in the right track for the spot from which they had started, they altered their course and turned in another direction.

The air had now become bitterly cold, which, added to the darkness, made the travelling doubly disagreeable, and Gordon Romilly, whose hands and feet were becoming quite numbed, felt sorry when his brand had burned itself out, and he was deprived of the warmth which it afforded him. But, by this time they had arrived at a large sholah, in which the "shikarries" found a quantity of dry bamboos.

"These are just what we want!" exclaimed Major Powell, "now we shall get on famously; the men will make some first-rate torches by tying a bundle of bamboos together, which will light us from here to the bungalow with ease."

He spoke cheerfully, although he did not feel so, and he and Romilly busied themselves in helping the natives to bind the bamboos together, which, when lighted, really produced a very fine effect; and the unexpected discovery put the aide-de-camp in such good spirits that, torch in hand, he commenced to cut some boyish capers amongst the brushwood, thereby endangering the safety of the whole.

"Take care, take care," called out the Major. "At this season of the year the sholahs are like tinder, and one spark will set the whole of it alight."

The words were no sooner out of his mouth, than Captain Romilly's torch, being carried aslant, came in contact with an unusually dry bush, and in a shorter time than it takes to relate, the thicket was on fire, and the four men had to run out of it as quickly as they could. They had hardly left it sufficiently behind them for safety, before the entire brushwood became a mass of flames, and there was a splendid bonfire, the dry wood crackling with successive sharp reports like that of musketry, and the flames rising high above the sholah into the night air.

"That was a sharp retreat," said Major Powell, laughing, as they stood and watched the burning brushwood. "The torch you've lighted for us, Romilly, ought to be bright enough to guide us home."

They stood and watched the blazing sholah until the fury of the fire was exhausted, and the burnt and blackened bushes had fallen, one by one, into the general *mêlée*, and left nothing behind them but a heap of calcined ashes. Then they turned away to remember, with fresh perturbation, that they were miles from the Avalanche Bungalow, and that the rapidity with which they had been compelled to quit the burning thicket had left them still more at a loss to imagine to which point of the compass they might be steering.

"There is no help for it, Romilly!" said the Major, without making any further attempt to conceal his alarm. "We have got into a terrible scrape, and the only thing left for us to do is to keep moving as cautiously as we can in one direction, wherever it may lead us, for there is no possibility of determining the right one. We may, by good chance, hit on our own road; but if we don't, we must walk till daylight, for it will never do to sit down or stand still in the terrible cold of this night air."

The prospect was not a pleasant one; but Englishmen are not given to lamenting in the face of real danger, and natives are very patient under misfortune, particularly when they have a good example before them; so that the little party plodded on almost cheerfully, and tried to make as light as they could of the disagreeable position in which they found themselves. But when they had almost given up hope of reaching any shelter before morning, and resigned themselves to the idea of walking in single file until daylight; when Major Powell's feet were so blistered that he could hardly take a step without pain, and Captain

Romilly's were so numbed with the cold, that he scarcely felt what he was treading on, the older and more experienced of their " shikarries " declared that he heard something, and entreated them to halt. Only too thankful to admit a hope of succour, they obeyed him gladly, and the man, after having listened steadfastly for a short time longer, gave a prolonged " hilloo," which, after a moment's pause, was answered from above them.

"Was that a voice, or was it echo?" asked Captain Romilly, doubtfully.

" A voice, my dear fellow! Don't you see that dull light coming over the hill towards us? We have most likely fallen in with some herdsman seeking his cattle, who will be able to direct us into the right path. Thank God for it! for I had begun to fear we had not seen the worst of our night's adventure."

" What the devil are these?" exclaimed Romilly, as two huge heads, with long, twisted horns and glaring eyes, suddenly appeared across their path, and seemed anxious to dispute the narrow way with them.

"Only buffaloes, Romilly; but take care they don't push you over the edge. They probably belong to the man who answered us just now. Yes! see, here he is!"

And as Major Powell spoke, a figure bearing a horn lantern came up with the shooting party, and carelessly thrusting his cattle to one side, placed himself in front of the sportsmen. As he swung his lantern over the group, the gentlemen could see that he was a tall athletic young native; but differing from his race in ordinary by wearing his hair cut like an European's, and being dressed in corduroy trousers, a flannel shirt, thrown open from his broad, well-covered chest, and a soft felt hat, which had attained no shape in particular. In one hand he bore a thick twisted staff, with the other he held the handle of his lantern, and as the light fell on his face, it shewed an honest kindly countenance, the smile on which disclosed a set of dazzling teeth. Major Powell began explaining their plight to him in Hindustani, though rather doubtful whether the herdsman would be able to understand him through that language; but when he answered, to their infinite surprise, he spoke in perfect English.

"From 'Buffaloes' Swamp' to the Avalanche Bungalow? Why, gentlemen, you are miles out of your way! You have been walking backwards all this time, and are much nearer Ootacamund than you are to the bungalow. It would take you hours to get there, if you could do it at all to-night, which I very much doubt."

"But what on earth are we to do, then?" demanded Major Powell, his surprise at the herdsman's address swallowed up in renewed anxiety, "we can't remain on the hills till morning, we shall be frozen to death!"

"If you will take such shelter as we can give you, sir, Père Joseph will make you heartily welcome to it! Our cabin is not twenty yards further on, and there you will obtain rest, if nothing else, till you can pursue your way."

"We shall be but too glad to accept your

offer!" replied the Major and Captain Romilly, who felt at that moment as though they would be thankful to be quartered with the buffaloes, and filled with curiosity to learn who their new acquaintance might be; their spirits raised by the unexpected relief which had come to them, they followed closely on the young herdsman's heels, whilst he further excited their surprise by apostrophising his milch buffaloes as "Célestine," and "Philomèle," and telling them to "*Allez donc!*" and "*prenez garde!*" as they stumbled over the precipitous paths which led to the abode of Père Joseph.

CHAPTER V.

PÈRE JOSEPH.

AFTER the lapse of a few minutes, the sportsmen felt that the path beneath their feet had become wider and more trodden down, and Célestine and Philomèle having suddenly dived into a rough shed which appeared upon the right, their conductor held up his lantern to show them the entrance to a sloping garden, planted on the side of the hill, and surrounded by stout palisades; on traversing which they came upon a small wooden-built house, having a verandah in front of it, paved with brick and covered with creepers. They had scarcely entered within these precincts, before a light was shown at the open door, and an old man appeared on the threshold, and called out—

"*C'est toi! n'est-ce pas mon fils? comme tu viens tard.*" To which David replied—

"*Oui! mon père, c'est moi, et je ne suis pas seul.*" And then, changing his language, continued: "These gentlemen have lost their way on the hills, Père Joseph, and I have brought them home until the morning. They are half-perished with the cold, and have had nothing to eat since noon. It is most fortunate that I met them. Had the cows not strayed beyond their usual ground to-night, I should not have come across Monsieur and his friend."

"*Mon Dieu!* is it possible!" exclaimed the old man, as he peered scrutinisingly at the strangers. "Enter, gentlemen, enter, I pray you; you are welcome to everything that we can give you. And you have your servants with you also," observing the "shikarries" in the background. "How is it that they permitted you to lose your way?"

"It was not their fault," said Major Powell, as with Captain Romilly he stepped into the sanded sitting-room. "We had brought down an ibex, which proved too heavy for us to carry; and it took so long to skin the animal that the night had fallen almost before we were aware of it."

"And you encountered my son as he brought home his straying buffaloes. Well, the blessed Virgin is good, and watches over the safety of all her children. David, take the 'shikarries' round to the 'go-downs,' and see that their wants are attended to; and you, sirs, please to be seated, and make yourselves at home."

They did so, surprised meanwhile to hear a man of European blood claiming a native for his son, and curious to learn the truth of the connection between them.

The room in which they found themselves was poorly, but very comfortably furnished, and showed none of those traces of abject poverty which had distinguished the missionary's home the night before. The sanded floor was boarded and beautifully clean, the chairs and tables were substantial, and curtains shut out the draughts from the diamond-paned windows. In a corner of the room was a large old-fashioned eight-day clock; above the mantleshelf hung a crucifix, carved in wood; and against the wall, where a staircase led to the upper apartments, was a *bénitier* of holy water, surmounted by a little figure of the Virgin and a natural branch of yew. From these symbols of the Roman Catholic faith, the strangers turned to look at their host in the full light of the lamp, and were not surprised to perceive that he was evidently a priest of the same persuasion; for though, in the privacy of his own fireside, he had cast aside his official robe, and supplied its place by a loose linen blouse, the robe itself was hanging on a nail just behind his arm-chair; and the black skull-cap which he wore on his head was not sufficient to conceal his shaven tonsure. Meeting the eyes of his visitors, Père Joseph smiled and said:

"My house, sirs, is doubtless very different to what you have been accustomed; but, rudely built as it is, you will find it warmer than the open air. It is but a 'shanty,' as we should call it in Ireland, but it has sheltered my head now for many a long year, and will do so, I expect, till it needs a roof no longer."

"Have you been in Ireland?" exclaimed Gordon Romilly with interest. "I am of that country myself."

"Indeed, sir! Yes, I know it well, for I was stationed ten years in Ireland before I was sent out to India."

"But you are not English!"

Père Joseph smiled knowingly. He was a stout rubicund-faced man, with a roguish expression in his eye, particularly apparent when he felt amused.

"No, sir; by birth I am a Belgian, having been born in the town of Rôve; but I have not seen my native country since I was twenty-five years old; and it is now thirty since I came out to India, and twenty since I was sent to do duty on the hills. Ah! well, there was a time when I little thought I should end my days up here; but it might have been worse perhaps, so I must not complain."

"Have you been settled here so long as

that?" said Major Powell, who, with Captain Romilly, was busied in drawing the charges from his gun, "I wonder I have never come across your house before. How far are you from the cantonment?"

"Five miles, sir."

"That is a long way to walk in and out."

"We don't think much of five miles," replied Père Joseph, "but neither have we much need of the cantonment. My little chapel is close by, as you will see in the morning, and my people are scattered here and there upon the hills around us. They are but a handful, sir—scarcely worth saying the masses for; any preacher would have done for them; but what can a man do when he is under orders?" and here Père Joseph shrugged his shoulders, and heaved a weighty sigh of discontent. "But I must keep you fasting no longer, gentleman. You must accept such supper as we can offer you, and believe it would be better if we had it."

With a bow which would not have disgraced a courtier, the priest rose from his chair as he spoke, and walking to the foot of the staircase, rapped twice with his stick, and called Véronique.

"That's not a bad idea of the old gentleman's," whispered Romilly to Major Powell. "I'm so hungry that I feel as though I should commence on him if he kept us waiting much longer."

"We're in for a regular adventure," was the Major's reply. "I wonder what on earth Newland and Romer will imagine has become of us."

"We're deuced lucky to have got here, I think," said Captain Romilly; "the priest seems a right jolly old fellow! I like him exceedingly."

Meanwhile, the summons of Père Joseph having produced no effect, he called again:

"*Véronique, mon enfant! où es tu?*"

To which a female voice replied—a voice which made Gordon Romilly turn his head to listen:

"*Me voici, mon père, que veux tu?*"

"*Descends, descends vite! voici des étrangers qui réclament nos secours.*"

As Père Joseph uttered these words, he turned and apologised to his guests.

"You will pardon my speaking French, gentlemen; but we are so used to do it amongst ourselves, that it seems difficult to express our meaning in any other language."

"I should not have guessed that you experienced any difficulty in talking English," said Gordon Romilly; "you speak it a great deal better than I do."

"Do you think so?" was the reply. "For myself, I find that I have never acquired sufficient ease and fluency in the English language; but my children speak it better than I do, although I taught it to them."

"How many children have you?" enquired Powell brusquely.

"You do not suppose I speak of my children after the flesh, sir," said Père Joseph smiling. "I am a Catholic priest. But those whom I call by that name are, the young man David, who conducted you hither, and whom I have reared from an infant, and my niece Véronique, my sister's orphan child, who has also lived under my roof since she was two years old. And here she is, gentlemen, to speak for herself."

The door, at the heading of the staircase, was flung open impetuously as he spoke, and a young girl appeared upon the topmost step, and stood still for a minute regarding the strangers. She was slight and graceful in figure, with large blue eyes set in a fair oval face, and long black hair hanging in two plaited tails either side her head. In fact, she was the same girl who had wept over the missionary's child the day before, and whose general appearance had so impressed the usually indifferent Captain Romilly as to betray him into wondering who she was, and where she could have come from. She was clad on this occasion in a short blue petticoat, and a black stuff jacket, and round her throat was loosely knotted a white silk handkerchief, so loosely that it fell beneath a red rose which was carelessly pinned into her bosom.

As Gordon Romilly looked up from the cleaning of his gun and recognised her, he would have given vent to an exclamation of surprise, had not she forestalled him, by first starting backwards to make a little gesture of astonishment with her hands, and then flying down the stairs to take up her stand in front of him.

"*Tiens!* they are the same gentlemen whom I met yesterday; ah, no! not both, but one. *You* are the same, are you not?" appealing to Gordon Romilly, "I told Père Joseph I should know you anywhere by your *belle chevelure. Mon père,*" she added, turning to the priest, "this is the monsieur who helped me to carry *la pauvre petite* on to her bed. Ah, what a sad sight, and what a terrible! Could you drive it from your eyes all the night long?"

"Hardly," he replied, as he saw her blue eyes glisten with tears; "do you know the family very well?"

"No, Monsieur! they are not my *intimes*, but I have often passed that way and made friends with the little children; and when they told me what had happened, what could I do but go? And the poor mother!

Ah, it was a scene to frighten one!" brushing her hand across her eyes as she spoke.

"*Tais-toi*, Véronique! I will hear no more of the death of that poor little heretic!" cried her uncle; "thou hast spoken of nothing else all day, and if thou canst not change thy subject, thou wilt give me what these gentlemen here would call 'the blue devils.'"

"*Les diables bleus! qu'est ce que cela veut dire?*" exclaimed Véronique, laughing through her tears.

"Keep thy questions till after supper," replied Père Joseph. "These gentlemen have been fasting since noon, having lost their way on the hills, and are ready for whatever thou canst give them. So be quick!"

"Oh, are you hungry?" she said earnestly, still addressing herself to Captain Romilly, "we have *potage*, Monsieur, and curry, and rice, and cheese, and perhaps a salad, and—"

"Get thee gone and make it ready!" exclaimed the old priest in a serio-comic tone, and then as the girl flew into the back of the house, calling "David" authoritatively as she went, he continued: "a woman's tongue is the only horse that never tires. They would feed you with words, lodge you with words, and clothe you with words: and words are things that a man likes only when he is well fed, well lodged, and well clothed."

"It would take a great deal of starvation to make one quarrel with such words as your niece's," replied Gordon Romilly: and then Major Powell asked him where he had met the girl before, and rather unwillingly, and with very little detail, he related their adventure of the previous day.

Much sooner than the Englishmen expected it, the supper made its appearance, by the hands of David and Véronique. A smoking bowl of vegetable soup, a dish of curry and rice, salad, cheese, and bread, formed a repast on which the hungry guests fell with appetites that charmed their hospitable entertainers; but it was some time before Captain Romilly could persuade

Véronique, who was hovering about his chair, to take a seat at all, and when she did so, she shyly rejected the one which he had set beside his own, and took up her station on a little stool by the knee of her uncle. But the young man David shewed no such bashfulness; he was a wonderfully fine specimen for a native, having a figure as muscular and well-built as that of an European, and possessing with it the regular features and singularly fine eyes of the Hindoos. His complexion was very dark, but his manners were as easy and unconcerned as those of the priest and his niece, whom he had evidently been brought up to consider his equals. He conversed as familiarly with the gentlemen, even more so than they had done, and had it not been that his eyes followed every movement of Véronique with ill-concealed admiration (a circumstance which Gordon Romilly was quick to discover, and inwardly resent), it might have been said that he treated the girl as much like a sister, as the priest treated him like a son. As soon as the meal was concluded, David, by order of Père Joseph, placed a large stone bottle of whisky on the table ; and Véronique having produced glasses and hot water, the priest begged his visitors would make themselves comfortable, and set them the example himself, by lighting his pipe, a proceeding in which he was speedily imitated by Major Powell and David.

Only Captain Romilly professed to be disposed for neither tobacco nor whisky and water, and under cover of the general dissipation, managed to approach nearer to Véronique, and carry on a bantering conversation with her, in a voice so low that the others could not catch the meaning of his words. He commenced by addressing her in French, and so delighted was she to find that he could converse in her favourite language (although he spoke it very indifferently), that her shyness melted away, and she kept on answering his questions, now with a light laugh at his mistakes; and then, in a tone of incredulity at the fervour of his compliments—until, indeed, the parley was made public by her exclaiming, in a voice of pleasure—

"*Ecoute, mon père! Monsieur a découvert que je ne suis pas Belge.*"

"*Et comment?*" demanded the priest, smiling.

"*En regardant mes yeux*—by my eyes!" she added, perceiving the comprehension was not general, for Major Powell did not understand a word of French. "Monsieur says that my eyes are English, and would betray me did I never speak a word of that language."

"But Monsieur is mistaken," said her uncle, smiling; "thine eyes are Irish, Véronique; there is not a drop of English blood in thy veins."

"Is Mademoiselle Irish?" demanded Captain Romilly, "I could have sworn it, without asking."

"Her father was," replied Père Joseph. "Her father was a brave good man, an Irish soldier named Thaddeus Moore, who fell fighting for his country in the Affghanistan war; and left his Irish eyes to his daughter, the only things he had to leave her, *le pauvre homme!* Thy father's eyes were the same as thine, Véronique—blue and saucy : there is not a thing in thee to remind me of thy mother, my poor Justine, except it be thy useless hands and feet."

Here the girl put out her small hands and feet, regarding them with comical compassion, and her blue eyes looked saucy enough as she pinched Père Joseph on the side of his cheek, and asked him what he would do for his breakfast and his dinner and his supper, if those "useless" members were not at his beck and call. As Véronique carried on this little *badinage* with her uncle, Gordon Romilly looked at her animated face with unfeigned admiration. She was like an April day, easily moved to tears or laughter, and he saw that she had inherited the Irish character with the Irish face.

Major Powell, under the combined influences of whisky and fatigue, had now fallen fast asleep in his chair, and with his limbs stretched out and his head well back, was making "night hideous" with his snores.

"It is time that we were all in bed," observed the priest, as a louder snort than usual from the slumbering Major surprised the little party into a laugh. "These gentlemen must be in need of rest. Shew the Captain to his room, *mon enfant*, and the other Monsieur must take the little *cabinet* on this floor. David and I will sleep together to-night."

No expostulation on the part of his guest being able to shake this hospitable determination of the priest, Captain Romilly consented to be shown to his room, and attended by his pretty handmaid, rose to say good-night. As Véronique, with the lighted candle in her hand, stepped on the stairs, she dipped her finger in the *bénitier*, and crossed herself, murmuring some words of prayer; and Captain Romilly, hardly knowing why, but certainly more for curiosity than any other feeling, followed her example, so far as touching the holy water was concerned. He thought that his action was unnoticed, but Véronique perceived it readily, and turning on the staircase, called to her uncle in a tone of real excitement—

"*Mon père, mon père, il est de notre réligion: vois donc comme il prend l'eau bénite.*"

"I rejoice to hear it, my son!" said the old priest, in a gratified voice. "I hoped it might be so, but almost feared to ask. The Holy Catholic is the Irishman's true faith."

"*C'est vrai, n'est-ce pas?*" said Véronique, appealingly.

"*Mais oui—je suis Chrétien,*" replied Captain Romilly, dubiously.

The moment he had uttered the words, he knew that he had unintentionally told a falsehood. He had meant to tell the girl that he was as much a Christian as herself, and that the outward distinctions of their faith signified nothing; but his French was not equal to the emergency, he stopped short because words failed him, and when he saw the universal gratification he had given by the confession of what he was *not*, he had not the moral courage to retract his avowal, and explain in English the mistake into which they had been led. And when he found himself in the passage above, alone with Véronique, and she turned her blue eyes, now softened by feeling, upon him, and whispered : "*J'etais sûre que vous n'etiez pas hérètique*," he felt still less capable of undeceiving her. And, after all, he argued to himself, it mattered little. His night's shelter over, he should probably never see the inmates of the priest's cottage again ; or if he did, it would be under circumstances of far less familiarity, and if it pleased them to consider him a Roman Catholic like themselves, the innocent delusion could not possibly hurt anyone.

The bed-room into which Véronique now ushered him was spotlessly clean, and he lay down between the sheets with an assured conviction that he should not open his eyes again until daylight. But the varied incidents of the past day prolonged their influence through his sleep, and some little time after he had retired to rest, he was suddenly roused from a night-mare dream of falling over precipices, and being whirled round and round in unfathomable darkness, by a sharp grating noise (like the bark of a mammoth watch-dog with a sore throat), which sounded close against his window panes, and, as it seemed to him, almost in his ears. Startled from a deep sleep, and quite unable to conceive whence the sound proceeded, Captain Romilly sat up in his bed, and shouted the first name that came into his mind.

"Powell! Powell!" he called out, without having the slightest notion whether his friend were sleeping above, below him, or at his side. No answer, however, was extracted from the Major, who was then blissfully unconscious of all external things; but after a few moments' delay, a slight rustle was heard in the passage, and a timid knock sounded on the bedroom door.

"Monsieur, Monsieur, is anything the matter? Did you call?"

The voice was Véronique's, and she had

opened a little bit of the bedroom door, that he might hear it more plainly. She spoke so quietly, and so entirely without alarm, that Gordon Romilly only remembered that he had heard a strange noise, and called out, like a great frightened schoolboy, and felt very much ashamed of himself.

"It is nothing," he stammered, "I am so sorry I disturbed you, Mademoiselle. But I have had bad dreams, and when I woke some animal made a noise close to my window, and startled me!"

"I daresay it was the samber barking," she answered, cheerfully, "they try to get into the garden at night, Monsieur, and steal the vegetables; but we have a stout paling, and they cannot possibly break through it. In a wooden house like this, one hears everything so plainly."

"I am really very sorry," apologised Romilly. "I ought to have known better, but—"

"It is nothing, Monsieur. I hope you will not be waked again; but if you want me or David, you have but to call : *Mais n'ayez pas peur : le bon Dieu qui nous protége ne dort jamais.*" With which words the door quietly closed again, and she was gone.

CHAPTER VI.

ON THE TRACK OF THE TIGER.

No further disturbance interrupted the tranquillity of Captain Romilly's dreams, and he slept till so late an hour on the following morning, that when he descended to the lower room, Major Powell and David were already pacing the little garden together, and Véronique was standing in the bricked verandah, watching their proceedings and shading her eyes with her hand from the brightness of the early sun.

"*Bon jour, Mademoiselle.*"

The girl started and coloured.

"*Bon jour, Monsieur*; look there!" and she pointed to a deep print in the garden mould before them, as large and as round as a small dinner-plate.

"And what of that?" asked Gordon Romilly, peering at the mark with eyes that saw nothing beyond itself.

"Why, Monsieur, it is the track of a tiger! you were right about the noise which disturbed your rest last night, and had we not all been very sound asleep we must have heard it too. No wonder the poor samber barked, and the cows must have been in terror also. The tiger's footprints are all round their shed, and he has walked the garden two or three times over. That is where he must have climbed over, Monsieur," pointing to a part of the palisades beneath which the earth and flowers had been much disturbed, "and he has broken my favourite rose-tree in his spring—the clumsy brute!"

"By Jove! you don't mean to say so!" exclaimed Captain Romilly, who felt quite uncomfortable on hearing in what close quarters he had been to the "monarch of the jungle." "It's very dangerous, you know, he might have got in at any of the windows, if he had chosen."

Véronique laughed, first turning her blue eyes upon him to make sure that he was in earnest.

"Oh! Monsieur, they never choose to attack, the poor creatures, unless they are very hungry. This one must have had his dinner, David says, or he would not have smelled round the cow shed without trying to enter it. David!" she continued, raising her voice, "*Monsieur est descendu.*"

At this the young native looked up, and raised his cap to Romilly, like a well-bred Englishman, and the Major quitted his side to approach that of his friend.

"Romilly," he said, pointing to the track of the tiger, "I expect this is the same gentleman who carried off the cow from the Avalanche Bungalow the night before last, and who has probably been sleeping off his debauch in some sholah ever since. I am going to stroll a little way farther, with David and the shikarries, to see if the trail is easily followed, for if so we must carry back the news to rejoice Newland's heart. Will you come with us?"

"Thank you; no, I think I would rather stay here," replied Romilly, his handsome eyes still half closed from the effects of his long slumber, "but when you've found him, Powell, if you'll let me know, I shall be charmed to make one of the party!"

"Indeed I shall do no such thing," laughed the Major, "since you won't take the trouble to look for him, yourself! You'd like your friends to do all the work, I suppose, and send for you just as the fun is going to begin!"

"Exactly, Major! you've hit it off to a nicety," said the A.D.C., "that's just what I should like."

"Well, you're honest at all events," replied Powell, "and so am I, in saying you won't get it from me. Come, David, if we are to do anything before breakfast, we must be off!" and in another minute the men had clambered over the fence together, and were stretching their legs in the sunshine across the breezy, pathless hills.

Captain Romilly stayed behind, in the verandah, and surveyed the scene around him. The dwelling of the Catholic priest, although like dozens of others on the Neilgherries, was so picturesquely situated and surrounded, as to attract his eye at once. The house itself, which was thatched and painted white, would have appeared common-place, had it not been for the natural beauties which adorned it, but its roof and sides were so clothed and wrapped about with creepers that scarcely a square foot of the building materials was left visible. Long, wreathing branches of honeysuckle and clematis hung from the top of the verandah, and trailed upon the shoulders of the girl who stood beneath them, and bushes of red and scarlet geranium set in the bed beside it, their gorgeous blossoms heavy with the morning moisture, reached higher than Captain Romilly's knee.

A fuchsia, covered with its crimson and purple bells, and a sweet-scented verbena, twined together above the porch, both plants having attained the height of six or eight feet, a growth which appeared almost incredible in Romilly's English eyes.

The long, narrow garden, which sloped away precipitately in front, was chiefly dedicated to the culture of vegetables, but all round the inside of the palisades had been set a hedge of various coloured roses, which were now in full blossom of red, and pink, and damask, and yellow, and white; and about which the little inhabitants of the beehives, placed in a sheltered nook at the corner of the enclosure, were wonderfully busy.

To the right of the dwelling stood the tiny Roman Catholic chapel, to which Père Joseph had made allusion the night before, but which would never have been recognised as such had it not been for the wooden cross surmounting its humble entrance. Far away as the eye could reach, all round the cottage, rising one above the other, stretched the verdant, billowy hills; with the exception of a couple of stacks of chimneys, just visible in the distance, the priest's house seemed to stand utterly alone, and as Gordon Romilly gazed about him, he thought he had never seen more isolated an abode.

"Monsieur will not fast any longer!" said the mellow voice of Véronique, at his side; and there she was with a cup of chocolate in one hand, and a plate of biscuits in the other, beseeching with her eyes, that the sultan would sit down and refresh himself.

"Many thanks, Mademoiselle! I am sure I am infinitely obliged to you, but are you not going to take any yourself?"

"I had mine, with the others, two hours ago," she answered, "but Monsieur slept late, and now, who is to know at what time they will return for their breakfast."

"Is your uncle not at home, then?"

"Père Joseph was called out to a sick person at four o'clock this morning, and he is so good he never delays to go—for the same reason, though, I hope he may be back the sooner! Oh! he is so good—so good! There is not a man on earth who is so good as Père Joseph."

She uttered this eulogium with clasped

hands and such evident faith, that Gordon Romilly, as he drank his chocolate, thought it must be very charming to be so believed in.

"And I ought to know," she added, fervently, "for I have known him all my life."

"Have you lived here very long?" said Captain Romilly, with somewhat of a shrug of distaste, as his eye wandered over the surrounding hills; "it must be horribly dull, sometimes."

Her face fell.

"Do you think so, Monsieur? I do not; but then I have never known another home, so I am not fit to judge; and I have so much to do, with my cow, and the garden, and the bees, that sometimes the days do not seem half long enough for me! Monsieur has not yet seen my little cow—she is so pretty and so gentle—I call her 'Erin,' because Père Joseph told me that is another name for Ireland, and I love Ireland, though I have never seen it."

"Were you born on the hills, Mademoiselle?"

"Oh, no, Monsieur; I was born in Bengal, but I cannot remember it. My poor mother was travelling with my father's regiment, in boats up the river, when I was born, and she was so ill that she died, and they threw her body over into the water. I was such a weakly little baby, and they had no milk to give me, so that everybody thought that I should die, too, but my father fed me with bread and water for five days, until they got to shore again, and he found a woman to attend to me—my poor, dear father! I wish that I could remember him!"

"How old were you when he died?"

"Only two years, Monsieur; and then a black woman brought me all the way over here to Père Joseph, and he has been my father ever since. And David was a big boy when I first came—he is five years older than I am, and he used to nurse me, oh, so kindly!—David has always been very kind to me."

"And how did David come to live with Père Joseph?" asked Captain Romilly, who had several times before wished to put the same question.

The expression of Véronique's eyes changed instantly from grave to gay.

"Oh! has not Monsieur yet heard how Père Joseph picked up poor little David one day when he was walking by himself—not here, but in the plains? He heard a faint cry coming from a small bundle by the roadside, and there, tied up in matting, was the poor little naked baby, half dead from hunger, which some wicked people had thrown out to starve and die. David says he hopes that it wasn't his mother who was so unkind to him, but he'll never find out now," said Véronique, shaking her head, "so what is the use of thinking about it. Père Joseph brought him home, and made a little Christian boy of him, and gave him me for a sister, and so I tell him, he must try and be contented. He is very nice, is David! strong and tall, and well-looking; does not Monsieur think so?"

She fixed her eyes enquiringly on him as she spoke; but on this theme Monsieur did not seem inclined to be enthusiastic. He acknowledged that David was a good specimen of his race, and ought to be very grateful to Père Joseph and Mademoiselle for all they had done for him; but he soon changed the subject, by asking Véronique if she had no wish to visit England.

"Yes! I should like to see England very much," she said, "if there were no sea between it and this country."

"Is Mademoiselle afraid of the sea then?"

"I cannot say that I am really afraid, Monsieur, because I have never seen it. But I dread the very thought of seeing it. I am tossing on it sometimes in my sleep, and it is always angry with me; it never rests or is peaceful."

He gazed up in her face astonished, as she spoke, and he saw that her eyes were fixed in a dreamy listless manner upon the boundless space around them.

"But those are dreams, Mademoiselle— they have no truth or substance in them. I have often crossed the sea myself, and I have never come to harm. If it does toss about a little sometimes, it is half in play: and our English ships are stout, and care nothing for a storm."

"Not always!" she answered quickly.

"Perhaps, not quite always; but it is a thousand chances to one if you meet with an accident. People are crossing the ocean every day, and the lives that are lost are few. You will not be such a coward when the time comes."

He spoke gaily, not supposing but that her fears were half-affected; but Véronique, taking his empty cup from his hand, turned from him with a deep sigh, and entered the house.

"Good morning, Captain!" rung the cheery voice of the priest, as he unlatched the garden gate, and advanced to meet his guest. "They tell me that we have had a visitor here last night, who may take it into his head to pay us the same compliment again, in which case it shall not be my fault if he does not receive a warmer reception than he met with yesterday!"

"You are a sportsman, then, *mon père?*"

"Well! hardly—or if I am I must not talk too much about it. There are people would deny a priest the pleasure of his dinner if they could. But being in these wilds, and subject to such intrusions as this one of last night, we are obliged to keep a few weapons in the house; and, having them, we take care, as in duty bound, that they do not rust—*voilà tout*," and Père Joseph's roguish eyes twinkled with secret understanding as he spoke. "I met David with Monsieur, *votre ami*," he continued, "busy over their trail within a few yards of the house; but it is useless for them to think of tracking the tiger so near the place. He's far enough away by this time, you may depend upon it; these animals will travel miles in a night. Véronique, Véronique!" he shouted, as, having gained the shelter of his arm chair, he rapped on the table with a stick, "*dépêche-toi sers le déjeûner—les autres seront ici dans un instant!*"

Before the words were well out of his mouth, the steps of David and Major Powell were heard in the verandah.

"Romilly!" exclaimed the latter with glee, "we must be off directly after breakfast, and look up those fellows from the Avalanche Bungalow. I have great hopes that we shall be able to follow up the trail of this brute, and shall leave one of the 'shikarries' behind me for the purpose: but it would be a shame to go after him without poor Newland—added to which, they will probably be wasting their own time looking after us."

"Yes! I suppose it would be as well to let them know that we are alive," replied the A.D.C. "It's a deuced bore, though, isn't it, that one's friends will persist in being anxious on one's account, and all that sort of thing—because explanations, and so forth, take up so much of one's valuable existence."

"Now, Romilly, do cut Bond Street and Buckingham Palace for once in a way, and attack these deer steaks like a rational being. These are samba, if I mistake not," he continued, addressing Père Joseph, whilst Véronique—who appeared to have shaken oft her fit of pensiveness—told Captain Romilly that he must taste them, because she had cooked them herself.

"Yes, sir, they are samba steaks," replied the priest, "and this curry is made of kid. We live chiefly upon deer and goats' flesh out here. Don't be afraid of Véronique's coffee, Monsieur; I taught her how to make it myself, and I'll lay you won't get a better cup in all India! That dish before you contains roasted sweet potatoes. You've come to a poor man's table, Captain, or you should be better treated; but such as it is, you are heartily welcome to it!"

They assured him, as indeed they might do, that they desired nothing better; and, the meal being concluded, Major Powell and Captain Romilly buckled on their shot-belts, and, throwing their guns over their shoulders, stood up to say farewell.

They shook the old priest heartily by the hand, thanking him again and again for his hospitality, in return for which they did not like to offer any more substantial proofs of gratitude; whilst Père Joseph assured them that never had visitors been more welcome to a host, and that if such poor entertainment as he could offer were not too humble for them, he hoped he might see them there again. The young native, David, refused to say good-bye, declaring his intention of walking back to the Avalanche Bungalow with them, lest they should again miss their way, and if they would permit him, of helping them also to follow up the tiger's trail, an offer which they gladly accepted. Only Véronique did not appear during these farewell moments. Captain Romilly's eyes sought her more than once, but she did not come, and no one seemed to miss her but himself.

Major Powell could not imagine why his companion lingered, when they had so much work before them, and when at last he persuaded him to proceed, he seemed to do it unwillingly. But as soon as Captain Gordon Romilly had placed his foot in the verandah his step was quickened, for there by the palisades stood Véronique with a bunch of roses in her apron, which she had gathered for him as a parting present.

"You said that they were pretty," she murmured bashfully as he came up with her, and took the flowers from her outstretched hand.

"How foolish of thee, Véronique, to wish to cumber Monsieur with a large bouquet, just as he is about to set out on a long walk," said David in a tone of reproach, which made the girl colour to her eyes.

"Give them back to me, Monsieur," she cried, as she attempted to reclaim her offering; "David is right—it was thoughtless of me to think that you could carry them."

"David is wrong," was the A.D.C.'s reply, as he held the roses far above her reach; "the flowers are mine, Mademoiselle, since you have been so kind as to give them to me, and I will resign them to no one."

He lifted his hat and turned away gaily with the bouquet in his grasp as he spoke; but if one might judge by the sudden crimson which rushed to his hearer's cheeks and brow, his looks had said more to her than his words.

The sportsmen's return journey to the

Avalanche Bungalow was unattended by any accident, unless being nearly knocked over by Romer, in the exuberance of his delight at seeing them again may be counted as one.

"My dear fellows! if I had brought with me a single pocket-handkerchief more than I shall absolutely need, I would weep with joy at your safe return—I would, 'pon my honour. If you hadn't turned up by dinner-time this evening, Newland and I had decided to go back into cantonment to purchase our mourning. We fully intended to appear at church next Sunday, like the Siamese twins, in complete suits of black glazed calico, made after the 'muster' of General Perkins. And, now here you have come back, and knocked our neat little plan completely on the head. Where have you been? what have you been doing? and why didn't you send us a letter by the post to come and join you? When four fellows agree to come out together for a little enjoyment, and two of them rush off and have the lark all to themselves, I call it an awful shame!"

"My dear Romer, when you've done talking, perhaps you will let us begin. If you consider it a lark to be tumbling in the dark amongst precipices, and risking your neck at every step you take, I wish you'd have let me know of it a little sooner, and you should have been quite welcome to my share of the pleasure."

"Why! you don't mean to say it's been so bad as that, Powell?" exclaimed Romer seriously.

"I do mean to say that we have had a very narrow escape of meeting with a bad accident, and if you'll call Newland, you shall hear all about it; but I never can persuade myself to tell a long story twice over."

"Not even when it's against her Majesty's Government?" said Romer slyly.

But as soon as the sportsmen had related their personal shares of the adventure of the previous night, for the benefit of their friends, and come to that part of it which related to the tiger's track, the danger they had undergone, the surprise first elicited at the mention of the priest's cottage, as well as the admiration for the ibex head and skin, were all alike forgotten in the eager delight manifested by both Major Newland and Captain Romer at the bare chance of being able to follow up and kill the thieving brute who had carried off the poor native's cow.

"Just fancy your having the luck to come across the beast in that way!" exclaimed the Major; "why, I sent my 'shikarry' out the whole of yesterday, and he could find no traces of him anywhere."

"Well, there are plenty of traces of him about the priest's bungalow, at any rate," said Powell; "and David, the young native I spoke to you of, who examined them with me, thinks we shall have very little difficulty in following up the trail, so I left the old 'shikarry' behind us to keep a sharp look-out till we come."

"Where's Daniel? Where's David? Where's Jehoshaphat?" cried Romer in his absurd excitement, "bring him in, and let us hear all about it. I shall neither eat, drink, nor take my rest, until the hour for starting and all the other preliminaries are arranged."

But on holding a consultation with the young native, it was decided that, as the day was already past its meridian, it was too late to think of going after the tiger until the next morning.

"I don't think he can be far from our cabin, gentlemen," said David, as he stood respectfully before them with uncovered head; "because his footprints were so fresh when I first saw them, that I expect he crossed our garden as he was looking for shelter after his night's prowl, and he is most likely lying down in one of the sholahs round about. He *may* move further on this evening, but if he does, your 'shikarry' ought to be aware of it, but I have known them lie for two or three nights in the same place when they have been well filled. If we went after him this afternoon, it would be growing dusk before we reached his lair, and it would be very dangerous to beat the sholahs after dark; so, if you'll take my advice, sirs, you'll go to bed early and be up with the sun, ride on horseback as far as our place, which you can easily do if I show you the road, and from there we will go after the brute on foot."

"But what will you do, David, if we ride?" asked Major Powell.

"I will borrow a 'tat,' Monsieur; there is one belonging to the man in charge of the bungalow."

And so it was agreed that they should follow David's advice, and be ready for a tiger-hunt the first thing in the morning, and Romer and Newland insisting on the young native sitting at the dinner table with them—a proceeding which, notwithstanding his European education, made him terribly uncomfortable—they brought him in amongst them, and made merry with him for the remainder of the day.

CHAPTER VII.

AN AWKWARD TUMBLE.

"Would it be impossible for Monsieur to procure any other animal to ride this morning?" asked David, as he watched Captain Romilly tightening the girths of his horse's saddle, and observed how restive the Arab became under the operation.

"Why do you ask?" said Romilly, curtly. He had not taken the same fancy for the young native as his friends, and was rather disposed to resent the intimacy they had established with him.

"Because the road by which we shall travel is very narrow, Monsieur, and in parts broken. A spirited horse is never a safe mount for the Neilgherry Hills; a pony is much more sure-footed, and less apt to shy. I would not venture to ride anything myself but a pony over the paths we must cross to-day."

"You may ride a pony, or a bullock if you like," replied Gordon Romilly; "but I wouldn't mount one if I had it. I have ridden this horse ever since I have been in India, and I never found him refuse to go at anything, yet. When I mount an animal, I become the master of it!" and with an air of supreme authority, the A.D.C., (who was as conceited of his horsemanship as he was of most other things), flung himself into his saddle, and sat there like a rock, whilst the Arab performed sundry curvets and other unnecessary exhibitions in front of the Avalanche Bungalow. David glanced at the fidgety animal for two or three seconds in silence, and then turned away without saying another word.

"We were so full of our exploits and adventures yesterday, Newland," observed Major Powell, as soon as the party was *en route*, "that I really believe we were egotistical enough never to enquire what kind of sport, in the meanwhile, you and Romer had enjoyed. Did you see any ibex?"

"Not one; for having sent off my 'shikarry' in search of the tiger, we did not feel competent to find our way over the hills without a guide. So we confined our explorations to the jungle at the back of the bungalow, where I brought down a couple of deer, and Romer got a good shot at a samba, and missed it?"

"But killed a wolf instead," said Romer, laughing.

"A wolf! why there are no such things here. If you had said a bear, I should not have been surprised!" said Major Powell.

"Well, it was as big as a wolf, anyway!"

"It was a wild dog," observed Newland, bluntly.

"There's Newland, as usual, calling himself a friend, and trying to put my light out. There's not much difference after all between one of these wild dogs and a wolf, is there, David?"

"Not when you meet them in packs, Monsieur," replied the young man, who was mounted on a mangy " tat," or native pony, so low in height that the long legs of his rider nearly touched the ground. " I saw a large samba once pulled down by them as easily as though it had been a sheep or a calf."

" Did you really ; where was that ?"

" In the Annomally Forests, sir ! I had gone down to the plains for a few weeks, to have some shooting with a friend, and I lost myself in the jungle. I'm sure I don't know how it happened, for we had been together all the morning ; but in the afternoon we separated, and though I had ' blazed ' the trees as I went, I couldn't for the life of me find my way back to the place of meeting. I fired shot after shot from my gun, in hopes that my friend would understand the signal and answer it ; but I heard nothing in return, except the occasional distant crack of his rifle, which seemed to go farther from me, the more I wandered about after its sound, till at last all my own ammunition was expended, and the night was drawing on so fast, that the only thing left for me to do was to climb up the straightest and most difficult tree I could find, in hopes of remaining safe in its branches until the morning."

"What a deuced uncomfortable position!" exclaimed Romer.

"It was so, Monsieur; I can assure you, I never wish to be placed in such a one again! As the daylight faded away, (which it quickly does in so densely wooded a situation), the forest became alive with hideous noises, and what with the darkness and the peril, I felt as though I were already in purgatory. All the animals of prey, the tigers, cheetahs, hyenas, and jackals, left their hiding-places, and prowled about, calling after each other, or howling for their own amusement; and more than once my heart nearly stopped beating, as I heard a rustling about the foot of the tree in which I sat, and felt (for the darkness was so great where the shadows fall, that I could not see), that some brute had smelt me out, and was making up his mind whether it would be worth his while to clamber up and fetch me down, or not."

"Good heavens! how horrible!" said Major Powell. "David, I wonder your hair is not grey."

"Should that have turned it grey, Monsieur?" said the young native, laughing, as he ran his fingers through his coal-black curls. "I don't think it has; but I never passed so long a night before! I am sure that forty-eight hours of ordinary darkness could not appear longer than those twelve did to me."

"Go on, go on!" cried Romer, impatiently.

"Well, Monsieur, I suppose it must have been about the middle of the night, when I saw the scene I mentioned to you. I had half fallen asleep, through weariness and fatigue, when I was roused by a most horrible noise, as if all the fiends in hell had been let loose about the forest. Yelping, snapping, snarling, whining, on it came like a torrent of sound, and just as I was wondering from what animals it could possibly proceed, there was a crash and a burst through the jungle near the tree in which I was concealed, and right before it, just in the line of the moonlight, flew panting, an enormous samba, with its head thrown back, its tongue thrust out, and its flanks literally bathed in sweat; whilst before it, around it, and on its heels, rushed a pack of these wild dogs. There must have been a hundred of them, if there was one. They were leaping at its throat, rushing between its feet, and hanging on its hinder quarters, and I was not surprised, the moment after the yelping crew was out of sight, to hear a heavy fall and a long moan, and to know that the poor samba had succumbed to its pursuers. I heard the devils through the darkness, tearing the flesh off its quivering carcase; and I was thankful, gentlemen, that it took place out of my sight, for to listen to it only made me feel quite sick."

"I don't wonder at it," said Major Newland. "I had no idea these creatures were so powerful. And did you remain in the tree till daylight, David?"

"Yes! Monsieur, I had no alternative. I saw several things that night that made my blood creep, considering that I had neither shot nor powder left. At one time, two tigers gambolled together under the tree like a couple of cats for more than half an hour, whilst I was dreading every moment lest they should smell me out, and turn their play into business; and at another, a huge elephant scratched his back so vigorously against the bark of it, that he nearly shook me out of the branches. But, thanks to the Blessed Virgin, nothing was suffered to molest me, though when the sun had risen, I was so cramped from sitting all night in one position, that I had hardly strength to leave it."

"There are a great many elephants in the Annomally Forests, are there not, David?"

"Hundreds, Monsieur, it is famous for them! Has not Monsieur heard of the young English officer who was killed there by one, about this time last year?"

"He means poor Williamson!" interposed Major Powell. "He held one of these appointments for looking after government timber, and spent almost all his time out in the Annomallies, shooting elephants. I can't tell you how many he shot in a year, the number was almost incredible. But he grew foolhardy with success, and at last took to going after them on foot, by which means the poor fellow lost his life, for having wounded an elephant without killing him, the huge brute wheeled round before Williamson could get out of his way, and crushed him to death."

"I thought elephants turned so slowly, that it was always possible for a man to avoid them if he were careful," remarked Newland.

"Not always! they turn slowly, it is true, but they cover an immense deal of ground, and should never be hunted except on horseback. A wounded elephant is the most dangerous of animals, for nothing destroys life more effectually than the pounding of their ponderous feet and knees. When poor Williamson's body was rescued from the one in question, there was neither shape nor consistence in it!"

"And was the brute killed eventually?"

"I believe not! To kill an elephant on the spot you must send your bullet through the socket of his eye, for they have been known to flatten against his frontal bone, and it requires an experienced shot to do that. Williamson's followers were probably too much occupied in collecting all that remained of their poor master, to think of looking after the animal that had destroyed him. It was a dreadful accident."

"But what was the end of your adventure, David?" demanded Captain Romer, "why hadn't your friend sent some one to look after you?"

"He had, Monsieur, both sent and searched himself, but when the darkness fell, they were as fearful to walk about the jungle as I should have been, for it is so thick there, that it is impossible to say at one step, what you may not meet the next. They sat up all night, however, in hopes I might come home, and in great distress lest I had been devoured; and as soon as the day dawned, they were on the search again, and I could hear their guns being fired in every direction, although I had nothing except my voice wherewith to answer them. I had watched the sun rise by that time; I had seen all the cowardly beasts of prey, the tigers, hyenas, and jackals, skulking home after their nightly prowl, as if they were terribly ashamed of themselves; and the gentler animals, the elephants, samber and spotted deer, going to browse on the outskirts of the jungle before the hot sun should have sucked up the moisture from the herbage; so I was no longer afraid to descend from my resting-place, and what with the reports from the fire-arms and my own shouting, my friend and I managed to get nearer one another, until we met. We were very glad to see each other, gentlemen, as you may suppose; and I was very glad to get into a bed the next night, and leave the elephants and tigers to their enjoyment without me."

"I should think you must have been," said Romer. "David, is that your home that we have just come in sight of?"

"Yes! Monsieur, that is the house of Père Joseph; and beside it, you see, stands our little chapel."

"By Jove! how pretty! You must let me come and pay you a visit, David, before we go back to cantonment, for I shall not be out this way again before my leave is expired." And then as the party of horsemen drew nearer to the priest's cottage, he continued, "And is that your—your—sister, who is leaning over the palings and looking in this direction?"

"Véronique is not my sister, Monsieur," replied the young native quickly.

"She calls herself so, at any rate," interposed Captain Romilly, who was near enough to have heard the remark, and noted the readiness of its answer.

"She may call herself so, Monsieur," replied David quietly, "because she knows no better title; but for all that, Véronique is not related to me in any way."

"One might easily see that, by Jove!" said the A.D.C. scornfully; at which remark Captain Romer threw him a quick glance of reproof, and the young native's cheeks flushed darkly; but neither spoke to him; and Gordon Romilly appeared perfectly indifferent to what they chose to feel.

"*Véronique! mon père, est-il à la maison?*" said David, as he rode a little in advance of the others; perhaps to better hide the discomfiture which had assailed him.

"*Non! il y a deux heures qu'il est parti pour la ville,*" came back in Véronique's rich, shy voice, but she was gazing meanwhile, not at her adopted brother, but a little further on, where the handsome, Saxon-haired A.D.C. bestrode his thoroughbred Arab; with a red rose, selected from her bouquet of the day before, conspicuously displayed in his button-hole.

"Shall we dismount and leave the ponies here, David?" demanded Major Powell.

"I think not, Monsieur. It is impossible to say how far we may have to walk. I think it will be best to ride as long as the road is practicable; and then send the animals back to our stable by the horse-keepers, to attend your return. But if you will wait a minute I will go round to our 'go-down,' and see whether the 'shikarry' may not be there, or have left some news of his whereabouts. Pray take care of your horse, Monsieur," he added, earnestly appealing to Captain Romilly, who was most unnecessarily reining in his Arab in order to make him perform sundry evolutions on his hind legs for the benefit of the blue eyes fixed upon him, "you have got the curb-rein a great deal too tight. He will have you over the side of the hill if you are not more careful!"

"D—n the fellow's impertinence! why doesn't he mind his own business?" exclaimed Captain Romilly, not quite *sotto voce* to Captain Romer; but the words were scarcely out of his mouth before the native's prophecy was fulfilled. A harder pull than before, in his impatience, at the Arab's tender mouth, made the restive animal (naturally resentful of the treatment he was undergoing) suddenly back towards the unprotected side of the narrow path, and in another moment he had reared violently upon a particle of loose earth, and, together with his thoughtless rider, fallen over the precipitous decline. A simultaneous exclamation from his friends, and a scream from Véronique, was all that Gordon Romilly heard, before he was whirled in mid-air and thrown with a violent crash against some opposing obstacle, which he had hardly had time to realise when an iron hoof, planted in his face, laid his forehead and part of his cheek open, and deprived him of all consciousness. The horse had fallen backwards, but providentially came against a clump of bushes in its descent; where, finding itself in a reversed and unnatural position, it had disengaged itself from its unfortunate master, by an unceremonious struggle and kick, which had rendered Romilly senseless, and caused the animal to roll still further down the hill, where it now lay bruised and injured, with its fore-feet entangled in the reins.

All above was now hurry and confusion. The sportsmen quickly dismounted from their steeds, and delivering them over into the charge of the natives, prepared with cautious steps, to go to the succour of their friend; but as Romer and Newland planted their feet upon the yielding, treacherous soil, they found that their intention was forestalled. Some one had already scaled the high palisades which surrounded the garden of the priest; some one had pushed everyone (even David himself) who attempted to interfere with her actions, to one side—and swift as a deer, and sure-footed as an ibex—rushed down the precipice to the assistance of Captain Romilly.

"Take care, Véronique; take care," cried David in their familiar language, as he anxiously watched the fearlessness with which, having gained the clump of bushes where the Englishman lay, she seated herself by his side, and placed his head upon her lap, " remember that with the shallow soil upon these rocks, the roots of the trees can have but little hold, and do not lean thy weight against them."

" I am safe enough !" she answered, hurriedly, " how canst thou think of me ? Quick, David ! fetch water, and something with which to stem this dreadful blood. He will bleed to death if thou dost not make haste !"

They all dispersed in different directions to try and find something which should aid the recovery of the A.D.C., and left her with him, for a space, alone. Meanwhile Véronique had tenderly placed a hand under his head, whilst with her little apron she strove to absorb the blood which welled freshly over his face as fast as she wiped it away : and her tears commenced to fall upon the unconscious stranger. Gordon Romilly certainly presented an appearance to frighten any sensitive beholder. His handsome nose and cheek had been severely cut by the horse's hoof, and being youthful and full of blood, the sanguineous stream flowed freely, and had dyed his bright locks crimson, and pretty well obliterated his comely features. And then to see a young, strong man suddenly deprived, apparently of being, is always an alarming sight: and Véronique's soft little heart quailed with apprehension at it. When Gordon Romilly awoke to consciousness again, it was to see a pair of dark blue eyes, eagerly searching his own to find some sign of life, and to feel hot tears slowly dropping at intervals upon his hands and face. He stared at her wildly for a moment, not knowing where he was, then half started from his recumbent position and gazed around him.

"I am all right, thank you," he said, hurriedly, as though in answer to some question. "I can go on now," and with the words fell back upon her lap, utterly unable to move.

"If you could manage to get to the top of the hill, with the aid of Véronique and myself, Monsieur," said David, who, armed with cloths and cold water, was also by his side, "I think it would be a good thing; for you must be very uncomfortable lying here."

He had descended to the help of Captain Romilly as soon as he had procured what Véronique desired him, and with her, had watched until he regained his consciousness. The A.D.C.'s friends had also been very anxious to go to his assistance, but David had entreated them to remain quietly where they were, representing to them that not being, like himself and the girl, accustomed to run up and down the precipices, they might meet with some accident themselves, and could not possibly be of any use to Captain Romilly. And so, considerably disheartened by the *contretemps* which had interrupted their sport, they were anxiously awaiting above, the moment when their companion should be able to rejoin them.

"Oh, I can walk well enough!" said Romilly, in answer to the native's last suggestion, "just stand out of my way, and I'll get up."

"Why should not Monsieur rest quietly here, until he feels a little stronger?" said Véronique compassionately.

"Monsieur can do as he thinks fit," replied David, who considered that the compassion was undeserved.

"Thanks, but I will go on, I am all right again!" said Romilly, with a look of gratitude at Véronique, and then he staggered to his feet, and placing a hand upon each of their shoulders, forced himself to climb the steep ascent down which he had fallen, and having accomplished it, without a sound to denote that he was suffering, sunk down upon the pathway in a deep swoon.

"Romilly!" Romer had just exclaimed, "will you be able to go on with us?" when Romilly tumbled down unconscious at his feet, "Good heavens! he has fainted! he will never be able to proceed, it would be folly to try."

"So it would, Sir," said David, "I dare say Monsieur is very much bruised, he has had an ugly fall. If you will kindly lift him up, gentlemen, and carry him between you into the house, Véronique will shew you what bed to place him on ; (*le lit qui est dans le cabinet du rez-de-chaussée, Véronique,*) and I will go and look after the poor horse, who, if I mistake not, is still more hurt than his master."

Newland, Powell, and Romer, did as he desired them, and preceded by the girl, whose face had re-filled with anxiety, carried Gordon Romilly into the cottage of the priest, whilst David descended to the succour of the horse. He found it in a deplorable condition, though not so dangerously injured as he had imagined. It had been much bruised and shaken by the fall, had an eye closed, and was lamed from the shoulder; but having led it gently down the remainder of the declivity, and brought it home to the stable by a more circuitous though easier path, he threw it down a litter of clean straw, and hastened into the house to enquire what news there was of its master.

Captain Romilly, having recovered from his faint, had been tenderly undressed by the kind offices of his friend Romer, and put into the bed which stood in a little room next the priest's parlour, whence he was now vehemently adjuring his companions to continue their search after the tiger, and leave him to take care of himself.

"I will take care of you, Monsieur," interposed Véronique, naïvely.

"I am sure you will, Mademoiselle, and it will be a great deal more than I deserve. It was entirely my own fault that I came to grief, and it will be a deuced shame, Romer, if you fellows let me spoil sport in this way. You'll force me to get up and remount that unhappy animal if you persist in remaining by my side; Newland, Powell, do say that you'll go on, and leave me here until I'm fit to follow you. Who knows what the rest of an hour or two, may not do for me?"

Notwithstanding all his conceit, and folly, and thoughtlessness, he had borne his pain, and now frankly confessed his fault so like a true Englishman, that his friends stood together cogitating, and could not come to a satisfactory conclusion about him. They wanted to follow up the trail of the tiger; but a new feeling was springing up in their breasts regarding the A.D.C., and they could not quite make up their minds to leave him behind, alone. First one, and then the other, proposed to keep him company, but Gordon Romilly put a decided veto upon each proposition, and declared his intention of remaining by himself or not at all.

"David!" he exclaimed, as the young native made his appearance amongst them, "persuade them to continue their hunt after the tiger! I shall never forgive myself if it is given up on my account."

"I see no reason why it should be, gentlemen," was David's consequent remark, "I am sure that Monsieur will be well cared for during our absence, and that the best things for him now, are rest and quiet. Père Joseph will be home in another hour, and see that he has everything he wants; meanwhile, he will be all the better for not talking, or being talked to.

We have plenty of time before us; and the old 'shikarry' is here, and tracked the tiger into a sholah about four miles off this morning, where in all probability he still lies. So that if you are agreed, gentlemen, I am quite ready to accompany you, and by the time we return this evening, I hope that Monsieur will be able to sit up, and listen to the account of your adventures!"

So it was settled that they should leave Captain Romilly as he desired, to recover the effects of his accident; and with many wishes for a speedy convalescence, the sportsmen filed out of the cottage door.

CHAPTER VIII.

SAINTE VÉRONIQUE.

THE fleshwounds received in his face, although very disfiguring, were the least part of the injury which Gordon Romilly had sustained. He had hurt his back very seriously in his fall, but unwilling further to interrupt the pleasure of his companions, had carefully concealed the discomfort he was enduring, until they should have taken their departure.

Now, considering himself alone, he thought it no longer necessary to place a restraint upon his feelings, and turning on his pillow gave vent to a deep groan of pain.

"Monsieur, Monsieur! are you suffering very much?" said Véronique, in a subdued, half-fearful voice, as she left her position in the sitting-room and came and stood by his pillow. He did not answer her, except by another groan, and the girl grew frightened. With the exception of an old native woman, who took the rougher part of the house-work off her hands, she was quite alone with him, and the dread lest he should again be about to faint, quite overpowered her.

Her tender bosom began to heave, and the tears rose freshly in her liquid eyes, as she stood, silently regarding him, with a look in which fear and compassion were marvellously blended.

"Is there *nothing* that I can do for you, Monsieur?" she demanded presently in a timid whisper, as she laid her hand gently upon his shirt-sleeve. Romilly raised his face from the pillow and stared at her.

"Are you there, Mademoiselle? I had really no idea of it. What must you think of me?" and he tried to smile, but bit his lip in the midst of the attempt.

"You are in great pain I am afraid, Monsieur!"

"Yes! confound it! I can't conceive what it is; I feel as though my back were being seared with red-hot irons. But I daresay it will be better presently! Do you know, Mademoiselle, how my poor horse is?"

"He is lame, Monsieur, but David says that a few days' rest will be enough to cure him."

Something in the tone in which these words were uttered, attracted Gordon Romilly to examine the face of Véronique; and then he saw that tears were on her cheek. The girl caught his look, and blushed beneath it.

"Are those tears for me?" he said quietly.

"Oh! Monsieur! it is so sad to see you suffer."

He put his hand out from the bed-clothes as she spoke, and held it towards her, and when she placed hers in it, he raised the little fingers to his lips. The action made Véronique turn scarlet; she snatched her hand away from his, so quickly that he could not distinguish whether the action arose from modesty or anger; and drawing it across her still wet eyes, ran into the next apartment. But it was not long before she heard his voice calling her again, and she could not but answer it.

"Mademoiselle! where are you?"

"I am here, Monsieur, close by; what is it that you want?"

"You don't know what pain I am suffering, nor how lonely I feel when you leave me here by myself."

"What can I do for you, Monsieur? Will you have a cup of coffee, or chocolate? or shall I put fresh bandages about your head?"

"No—no!—none of these! only come in here and sit down somewhere where I can lie and look at you; for the pain is twice as bad to bear when you leave me, all alone."

"Have patience for one moment, Monsieur, and I will do as you ask me; but I must get the meat and potatoes on the fire first, or we shall have no dinner to-day."

"What are you doing now, then?"

"Peeling potatoes, Monsieur!"

"Can't you bring them in here, and let me watch you peel them. It is so stupid with nothing to amuse me."

He spoke so like a fractious child that the girl, although she laughed at him, made no further objection to his request, but lifting the heavy wooden bowl which contained her potatoes, carried it, spilling water over the floor at every step, into the bedroom where he lay, and placed it on a chair beside him.

"Now, Monsieur, I hope that you will be satisfied."

"Thank you, yes! that will do very nicely, and you need not talk unless you desire it. I only want to have something just to look at."

This generous permission of silence accorded her by the A.D.C., had the effect of chaining Véronique's tongue altogether; and, washing, scraping, and peeling her potatoes, she stood by the wooden bowl for the next ten minutes without speaking a word, whilst Gordon Romilly kept his eyes fixed upon her changing face, as though he were studying her features with a view to reproducing them on canvas. Presently he said, and rather abruptly:

"Why were you called Véronique, Mademoiselle?"

"Because I was born on the ninth of July, Monsieur, which, as doubtless you know, is the day of the blessed Sainte Véronique Giuliani. I was christened Véronique Marie after her and the Blessed Virgin."

"Véronique Marie Moore," said Gordon Romilly slowly, as though wishing to impress the words upon his memory. "That is a very pretty name! And so Sainte Véronique is your patron saint, I suppose."

"Certainly, Monsieur, and which is yours?"

"I haven't one," replied Captain Romilly, forgetting he was supposed to be a Roman Catholic.

"Not any!" exclaimed Véronique, dropping the potato upon which she was engaged, in her surprise. "Not any, Monsieur; but how can that be? On which day were you born?"

"On the third of November," said Gordon Romilly, aware that he had got into a scrape, but not the least how he should get out of it, for of saints and saints' days, their peculiarities and obligations, he was utterly ignorant.

"The third of November," replied Véronique, "it is the feast of the blessed Saint Hubert. Are you not named Hubert, Monsieur?"

"I have no name but Gordon," said the A.D.C., ruefully.

"Gordon, Gordon," repeated the girl, pronouncing the syllables as though they were French. "I don't think there is any saint of that name. And Monsieur is sure he has no other!"

"Quite sure!" said Romilly, shaking his

head. "You see my friends were very negligent, Mademoiselle, and didn't care whether I had anybody to look after me through life or no."

"The Blessed Virgin and the saints protect you all the same," said the girl, earnestly; "but it is strange it should have been omitted."

"I must adopt a saint, Mademoiselle, if you do not think it is too late for me to begin. Which shall I take? you shall help me to a choice."

"St. Hubert is your proper guardian," replied Véronique, without an idea that he was jesting, "and you should have borne his name."

"But I prefer a lady guardian," said Captain Romilly, looking up into her eyes. "I shall take Sainte Véronique. Do you think she will look after me properly, Mademoiselle?"

The girl lowered her gaze to his, and saw that he was laughing.

"This is not a subject for jest, Monsieur," she said, gravely; and Captain Romilly had to groan several times, and talk a good deal about the pain he was enduring, before he could get her to look as interested and sympathetic as she had done before. As soon as the potatoes were ready, they were obliged to be carried away into the kitchen, and set upon the fire; and just as Véronique had assured the A.D.C. that in another ten minutes he should have his dinner the sound of horses' hoofs was heard, and Père Joseph's stout mountain pony ambled round to the stable door.

"Here is *mon père*," exclaimed Véronique, as she flew out of the cottage door to meet the priest, and before they re-entered it together, she had put him in possession of all that had happened since his departure.

"I am very grieved to see you like this, *mon fils*," was the greeting of Père Joseph to the prostrate A.D.C.; "but since you did fall, let us be thankful that it happened so close to the house. Véronique and I will take every care of you till you are able to move about again, which, for your own sake, I trust may be very soon."

"I am only afraid that I shall be such a trouble to you and Mademoiselle, *mon père*," said Captain Romilly, as he tried to turn himself, and made a wry face in the attempt. "I never intended to tax your hospitality like this; but they carried me in here, whilst I was still unconscious."

"And where else should they have carried you?" demanded the priest, smiling. "I only spoke for your own sake, Monsieur. You will not find Véronique or myself complain of the pleasure of your company, however long we may have it. But allow me to look at your back; I am a bit of a doctor as well as a priest, and have a famous stock of potions and liniments upstairs, made from my old grandmother's receipts. Ah! I see what is the matter with you," he continued, as he lifted the coverings, and discovered the young, straight spine, now fast discolouring from the effect of a mass of bruises. "It is very painful, without doubt, but there is nothing dangerous here, and a good rubbing, and a couple of days' rest, will set you all right. I am afraid your back will be mended before your face, Monsieur; you've spoilt your beauty for awhile, there's no doubt of that, and it's just as well that you're in the jungle, with no ladies to look at you;" and chuckling over his own remark, Père Joseph stumbled up stairs, to return with a huge bottle of liniment, which he insisted upon rubbing into Romilly's back at once, although the latter was most eloquent in his entreaties that he should wait at least until he had had his dinner. As soon as the meal was concluded, the good-natured priest fell to work again, and Captain Romilly found the effect of these continued lubrications so soothing, that when Père Joseph, fairly tired out, called to Véronique to bring his pipe and his arm-chair into the bedroom of his guest, the A.D.C. requested her to hand him his likewise out of the pocket of his coat, and the two men fell to smoking together.

"Ah! my grandmother was very famous for everything of the kind," remarked the priest in answer to an expression of gratitude on Romilly's part, for the good the liniment appeared to be doing him; "if anyone was sick in Rêve, they always came to her for the remedy, and believed in it much more than they did in the doctor's."

"Is Rêve a large place, *mon père?*" said Romilly.

"No, no, quite the contrary, though it appeared a grand place to me because I saw it through the eyes of youth. It is a small town on the outskirts of Belgium, and not far from the famous forest of Ardennes. Ah! they were happy days I spent at Rêve, Monsieur, I have had none like them since; and never shall again."

"The days of our childhood are usually the happiest," rejoined Captain Romilly, whose pipe had awakened in him quite a moralising mood, "when we have no dunning letters, nor tailors' bills, nor anything of that kind to bore and disturb us!"

"My troubles have not lain in the way of tailors' bills, as Monsieur may well believe," said the priest smiling, "but they have had the power to affect me nevertheless. I quitted Rêve with hopes of rising high in the profession I had chosen, and I have lived to see my hopes disappointed, and to find myself in a position little better than that I left behind me."

"You were ambitious, *mon père*," said Romilly knocking the ashes from his pipe against the bedpost.

"I was : I don't deny it, but the feeling was instilled in me. My father was a small *avocat* in the town of Rêve, and his greatest wish had always been that one of his three sons should enter the church. My eldest brother, Pierre, flatly refused to do so ; he took a wife from the *bourgeoisie* instead, and entered into partnership with his father-in-law ; the second, Henri, as soon as the proposal was made to him, ran away from home and enlisted in the

French army; there remained, therefore, but myself, *le pauvre petit Joseph*, to fulfil the wish of my father's heart. So, fearing I should follow the example of my brothers, he took me early in hand, and pointing out to me all the glory and honour of serving in the church, expatiated on how I might rise to wear the robes of a cardinal, and officiate in the grand cathedrals of our cities. I was shown all the pomp and splendour of the profession, Monsieur; I saw the priests in their gold and silver vestments, followed by their attendants and bowed down to by the people, and I thought as my father told me, that I should rise to be the same some day, and receive like honour. I little dreamt it would come to *this*," said Père Joseph as with a comical glance his eye roved round the barely furnished apartment, " and a darned black gown. However, doubtless it is for the best!"

"But how did you get so separated from all your people?" demanded Romilly.

"When a man has taken a vow of

implicit obedience, Monsieur, what can he do? I belong to the order of Jesuits, and I suppose those in authority had their own reasons for sending me out of the country, for try as I would, I have never been able to get back to it again. First, I was ordered to Ireland, and much against my wishes remained there for ten years, during which time my youngest sister Justine, who had joined me, married her soldier and followed him to Bengal; and just as I was hoping to revisit my own place and people, I was drafted out to India also, and have been here ever since. Thirty years is a long time to be expatriated, Monsieur!"

"It is, indeed," said Romilly, who could not help recalling his own impatience over an expatriation of three months, "and have you never seen one of your family since then?"

"Not one, Monsieur! except little Véronique there, who was born to her parents after ten years of wedded life, and cut short their happiness just as they thought it was going to be increased. But that's generally the way in this world."

"Have you made no efforts to rejoin your family, Père Joseph?"

"It is out of my power, *mon fils*, I am bound to do only as I am bid."

"But you are happy here, are you not?" said Romilly dubiously.

The priest shrugged his shoulders.

"I am contented, Monsieur; were I to say more I should speak falsely. My parents are dead—my brothers and sisters scattered—why should I now desire to return to a place where probably all is changed from when I knew it? But for one reason I could almost wish that my days might end where they most probably will, in this little settlement."

"And what is that?"

"Véronique, Monsieur; I cannot bear to think that when I die, Véronique shall be left alone in this country, to marry whom she will, or to live how she may. For the child's sake I would yet return to my native land; for my own, I would lay my disappointed hopes in the grave as soon as may be," and Père Joseph began to take long pulls from his pipe, and look more solemn than Gordon Romilly remembered to have seen him do before.

"*Mon père*, thou shalt not speak of the grave, nor anything so melancholy," said the caressing voice of Véronique as she came and laid her hands about the old man's shoulders. "Thou art not to die, nor anything of the sort; but to take me home to Rêve some day, and let me say a prayer with thee beside thy mother's grave. How canst thou talk so? Thou wilt make Monsieur have—what is it that thou callest them?—*les diables bleus*, if thou canst not find some more cheerful subject to discourse upon. And how is he to sleep, or take his rest at all, if thou talkest to him all the day?" and Véronique smoothed down Gordon Romilly's bed clothes, and changed the bandages about his head, with quite the air of a nurse who imagines that her patient has been injured by some meddling interference in her absence.

"*Eh! bien, ma petite,*" said the priest good-humouredly, as he rose from his chair and laid his pipe on one side, "if thou sayst it must be so, it must be so; and we will leave Monsieur to try and get a little sleep. Sleep will do you more good than any medicine, Monsieur, for your nerves have been shaken as well as your body, and nothing but rest will effect their cure. Try to sleep, and by the time your friends return I hope they will find you considerably better."

"*Dormez bien, Monsieur,*" said Véronique as she softly drew down the blind, and prepared to follow her uncle from the room, "*et que le bon St. Hubert vous ait en sa sainte garde.*"

Gordon Romilly would rather Sainte Véronique had remained to watch over him herself, for he was becoming more and more interested in the priest and his pretty niece; but he acknowledged the wisdom of their advice, and having lain for some little while longer, perfectly certain that he could never comply with it, suddenly dropped his eyelids over his heavy eyes, and became profoundly unconscious to all external things.

CHAPTER IX.

THE PROSTRATE A.D.C.

"HOLLOA, Romilly! here we are again; we've bagged the tiger and no mistake. How are you, old fellow? will you be able to come on with us, to-night?" shouted Captain Romer, with no manner of discretion, from the front of the priest's bungalow.

"*Silence, Monsieur! il dort!*" exclaimed Véronique, as, with her finger on her lip, she rushed out to quiet the intruder. Captain Romer understood the action, though he did not understand the words.

"I don't know what on earth you're talking about, Mam'selle, but can't I see Captain Romilly? is he worse?"

"He is asleep, Monsieur," replied Véronique, "and if you make so great a noise you will awake him!"

"I say Powell, Romilly's asleep!" said Romer, in not much softer a key, as he turned to his friends—

"No, I'm not!" thundered Gordon Romilly, through the closed door of his apartment, "Come in, Romer, I want to speak to you!"

He had been roused from his doze, which had lasted until five o'clock, by the vociferous greeting of his companion, and was at once all anxiety to hear what success had attended their day's undertaking.

"Oh! he's awake, it's all right," exclaimed Romer, as he jumped off his pony, and prepared to enter the bungalow, "I won't be a minute, Powell, but I must just see how the fellow is, and tell him of our luck."

"If he's awake, it is you who have waked him, Monsieur," said Véronique, as, slightly pouting, she walked back to her seat.

"Well, Romilly! how do you feel now?"

said Romer, as he entered the presence of the A.D.C. " Will you be able to go out with us after ibex to-morrow—it will be our last day, remember, and we want to make it a success."

" I wish I may be able to turn myself in bed by to-morrow," groaned the unfortunate Romilly, " I'm so stiff, I can hardly bear the weight of my coverings; and yet if I lie in one position for ten minutes together, I ache all over. But have you got the tiger?"

" To be sure we have; it was the most splendid thing you ever saw—I wish you had been with us, but I can't possibly wait to tell you of it now, I promised Powell I wouldn't stay a minute, for we've got some way before us, still, and he doesn't want to be benighted on the hills a second time. But to-morrow—"

" Oh! can't you stay a little longer?" said Romilly, in a voice of disappointment. " I want so much to hear all that you've been doing, and how you set about it!".

"Cannot we persuade you, Monsieur, to stay the night with your friend?" interposed Père Joseph, who had entered the room during their colloquy; "we have a bed at your service, if you will accept it, and you might join the other gentlemen at any place appointed, in the morning. Captain Romilly will be very glad of your presence."

Romilly's eyes said "stay," and Captain Romer only hesitated for fear of the trouble he should cause.

"I would stop, directly," he stammered, "only it must be such a bore for you and your niece to have a lot of strangers knocking about the place."

"Monsieur!" said Père Joseph, with that courtly air which he sometimes assumed, and which bespoke his foreign breeding, "you have but to glance round this wilderness, to believe me when I say that to secure the occasional company of one or two guests is a real luxury to us. I dwell in these solitudes because I *must*; not because I prefer it: and if you will consent to enliven them with your presence for a few hours, *we* shall be the debtors, and not yourself."

"Hang it! I can't refuse to stay after that!" whispered Romer to Romilly; so having given a brief explanation to his companions, and made an agreement where to meet them on the following morning, he returned to the bedside of the A.D.C., while Newland and Powell rode home to the Avalanche Bungalow.

"And now tell me all about the tiger!" said Romilly, as soon as they were together again, "Where is the brute? and whose shot brought him down?"

"I believe the honour is divided between us," laughed Romer, "but it was on this wise. After we had parted with you, this morning, the old 'shikarry' conducted us about three miles from this, and then we had to dismount and walk about a mile further on to where there was a large, thick sholah, between the cleft of two hills. The man declared that the tiger was lying asleep a few paces within the sholah, but

David said it was not safe for any one to venture in, and so he gathered some large stones, and threw them as far as he could into the bushes, to see what he could rouse by that means. We were all waiting outside, with our guns on full cock, but really not in the least expecting that the brute was so close at hand, when, after a larger stone or a longer throw than before, out he came into the very midst of us, with a spring like a huge cat. I fired at once, and it was very lucky I didn't kill somebody, for just as I pulled the trigger, that fool of a young 'shikarry,' with a yell of terror at the sight of the tiger, rushed against me, and knocked me right over on my back, upon a heap of stones. I was up again in a minute, but the poor brute was already disabled; Newland had put a bullet into his shoulder, and Powell another into his throat, and he was lying over on his side, panting, snarling, and lashing his tail at us. There was nothing left to be done but to walk up as close to his head as one dared, and put an end to his pain. It was all over a great deal too soon for me, but it was jolly excitement whilst it lasted. David had not the chance of a shot at him, and the only one of us who was hurt was the coward of a 'shikarry,' who tumbled over into a 'nullah,' in his flight, and 'barked' his shins in a most glorious manner."

"How I wish I had been there," sighed Romilly, "however, it's no use wishing. This confounded fall will cut me out of all enjoyment for the rest of our trip. How large is the tiger?"

"Not very large! about eight feet from tip to tail, but beautifully marked, and in prime condition—we are going to toss up for the skin, for we really don't know whose by right it should be—I hope I shall get it."

"I'd have a hunting suit made of it, were I you."

"Not I! a young fellow lost his life up-country some years ago, by that means. He had had a suit made of cheetah-skin, thinking in consequence to get nearer to his game, and one of his brother officers, catching a gleam of it through the jungle foliage, mistook him for a cheetah, and shot him dead. No tiger suits for me, thank you, Romilly! you'll be trying your maiden hand on me, if I do."

"It will be a long time before I try my hand on anything again, I am afraid," said the A.D.C., ruefully.

"Nonsense! you mustn't be so 'blue.' Shall I write home to your friends, and tell them of your precarious situation?"

"I wish you would! perhaps his lordship might be induced thereby to make a small addition to my usual allowance in order to defray the expenses of the doctor's bill!"

"Oh! if that's your game, why not carry the joke a little further, and say you're dead at once. I've heard of a scamp in these parts, who had got so much money out of the home powers, by constant representations of illness, that at last they refused to credit his assertions any longer, and only sent condolences in return for his pathetic letters. So, reduced to extremities, he got a friend to write to his hard-hearted relations, announcing his premature death, and requesting they would send a remittance to defray his burial expenses, which they accordingly did. What became of the gentleman after he had spent his funeral-money, I never heard, but I think he deserved to be supported for his ingenuity."

As they were amusing themselves over this anecdote, Véronique appeared at the door to announce that tea was ready, at which meal Captain Romer made himself so facetious, that David and the priest were soon laughing as heartily as Romilly had done before them, and the A.D.C., with his bed-room door open and his mouth full, almost forgot his aching bones as he joined in the general merriment. Only Véronique seemed to regard the new-comer with distrust, almost amounting to distaste : she was jealous of the inspiring influence he exercised over her patient, although she did not sufficiently recognise the feeling to acknowledge it to herself.

"Why does your friend call eggs 'hoofs,'

and say 'let's parley voo, Mam'selle,' every time I speak English to him?" she enquired with knitted brows of the A.D.C., as she brought him his second cup of coffee. "He speaks good English, and we can understand him; why doesn't he keep to his own language?"

"Because he wants to have some fun with you," replied Romilly, who was secretly pleased at the dislike she evinced to Captain Romer.

"I don't like that sort of fun," said Véronique, shortly.

"It isn't everyone who can speak such beautiful French as I can, you see," said Romilly, archly; "mine is pure Parisian, is it not, Mademoiselle?"

The girl cast down a smile upon him, a contradictory smile, but a very lenient one.

"You speak better than your friend!" she said, evasively.

"Now, *Moosoo*," cried Romer, as he stood up after his tea, "I feel all the better for your kind attentions. There's nothing like a good meal to make a man feel at charity with himself and the world; and I begin already to experience pricks of compunction for having helped to kill the poor tiger."

" Don't do that, Monsieur," said David, laughing, "for I warrant he would have had no compunction whatever at making a meal off you."

" Well, I suppose not, and who's to blame him? If there's one thing I despise above another, it is the man who can't eat himself, nor let his friends eat. It's very evident to me, Moosoo, that you don't belong to the same tribe as my friend Dr. Baddell, in the cantonment yonder, who cuts down the provisions for himself and his household so short, that he has been known on more than one occasion to be forced to eat his own words?"

" Ha! ha! Monsieur," roared the priest, " airy nourishment, upon my faith; but very hard to digest, sometimes."

" You speak truth, but what do you think of the digestive powers of his poor horse, whose allowance of 'gram' was diminished, day by day, until one night, rendered desperate by hunger, he first eat up the whole of his bed, and then devoured the 'joul' with which he was covered?"

"Like the rattlesnake in the Zoological Gardens, who swallowed her blanket," said Romilly.

"Exactly so, the only difference being that the blanket re-appeared after a few days' seclusion; but Dr. Baddell's 'joul' was never seen again!"

"How hot your head is, Monsieur," said Véronique, as she dipped Captain Romilly's bandages in cold water, and replaced them about his wounded forehead.

"It does ache a little," he said, wearily.

"There is too much noise and talking going on in the next room," replied the girl. "Let me close the door, Monsieur, and try to go to sleep again."

"No! no! I should not be able to sleep a wink at night," he answered, hastily. "The fact is, Mademoiselle, I present so ugly an appearance with these bandages about my head, that I frighten you, and you want to shut me out of sight."

She looked at him for a moment without speaking; then, pulling the bedclothes straight, and tucking them in at the side, passed into the next room.

These little quiet attentions on her part were very attractive to Captain Romilly; he liked to be thus taken possession of, and gently rebuked when he was forward, and coaxed into good behaviour when refractory. He had already begun to consider the attendance of Véronique about his pillow a necessary thing, to think the room looked empty when she was gone, and to feel himself more easy in her presence—and he excused the fact to himself on the score that women were born for nurses, and understood the art by intuition. But Captain Romer volunteered to be his nurse that night; he had stayed behind, he said, for the sole purpose, and refusing all offers of a comfortable bed, avowed his intention of lying down on the floor of Captain Romilly's room. It was in vain that the priest and David offered to sit up with the A.D.C. themselves, and that Véronique, who seemed most anxious that Romer should be ousted from his position, declared that the room was much too small for two people to sleep in, and that the patient could not possibly need any attendance. If they had not given him a mattress, he would have lain on the bare boards; and so, in deference to the rights of hospitality, they were compelled to let their guest do as he liked. But Véronique was so very particular in impressing upon Captain Romilly that if he wished his head to be any better in the morning, he must not talk further that evening, that as soon as the final goodnights were said, and the members of the priest's family had betaken themselves upstairs, her interference called forth some trite remarks from Captain Romer.

"I say, Romilly, what does that little French girl mean by looking at me as if I meant to eat you? What earthly difference can it make to her whether your head gets well or not? As if it wasn't of twice as much consequence to me as to anybody else. She's rather pretty when you can get a good view of her face, but confoundedly 'cheeky,' that's my opinion of her."

"Like all her sex!" responded Romilly, meanly evading the argument, like most of his, when a woman is concerned in it. "I daresay I'm a bit of a bore to her, lying here to be waited on, and she'll be glad to see me well enough to walk out of the cottage door; however, don't let's waste our time talking about her, Romer, I want to ask if you could manage to send over my things from the Avalanche Bungalow tomorrow, because I must have them if I'm to stay here a day or two longer."

"Is there any chance of that?" enquired Romer, with a lengthened face.

"Well, you see, I can't move; the question is how soon I shall be able to do so?"

"Won't you see a doctor?"

"Where would be the use? I'm only

bruised, and the priest's lotion will bring me round as soon as anything else."

"It's such a bore it should have happened so," said Romer, grumbling, "for I shan't have another chance of going out with you, Romilly. We must return to Ootacamund the day after to-morrow, and my leave will be up next week. Powell is going down about the same time, so we've agreed to travel together, and take a couple of days' shooting at Bandypoor on our way, and I had quite hoped you would have accompanied us so far; it's just at the foot of the 'ghaut.'"

"Vain are the hopes of man!" exclaimed the A.D.C.

"You seem to take it uncommonly quietly," rejoined Captain Romer, rather disposed to resent his friend's passiveness.

"How else can I take it, my dear fellow, tied hand and foot as I am? As soon as I can walk by myself again, I shall only be too glad to rejoin you anywhere; but till then, I suppose I am a prisoner here."

"Well, I've got to be up early, so I'll

say good-night to you," replied Captain Romer, ensconcing himself under his bed-clothes, when he was soon fast asleep.

Gordon Romilly could not follow his example; the unusual *siesta* he had indulged in during the afternoon had made him wakeful, and his aching back and burning forehead rendered him doubly so. He tossed about his narrow couch, groaning at every fresh movement, till he had rendered it thoroughly uncomfortable; and then, when he called Captain Romer to his assistance, they got the bed-clothes into such a puzzle between them, that they gave it up as a bad job, and ended by putting them all back in a heap, the weight of which was almost intolerable to the A.D.C.'s tender back and shoulders. He lay, lamenting his condition, and reviling Captain Romer's hearty snores, until the seemingly interminable night had passed, and the grey dawn appeared through the flimsy blind, which alone protected the little casement; and then he fell into an uneasy troubled sleep for a couple of hours, and woke to find that his companion had risen, and that the morning sun would have been streaming in upon his face, had not some one pinned up a dark cloth across the bed-room window. Some one also had arranged the bedclothes comfortably for him, and placed a sweet fresh rose, tied up with a sprig of scented verbena, upon his pillow.

Gordon Romilly had scarcely had time to note these changes, before the rustling which he made in turning, brought footsteps to the outside of his door, and he heard the voice of Véronique asking if she might enter, and as soon as he had given her permission, she stood before him with a cup of coffee in her hand.

"You have not slept well, Monsieur," she said, "I knew you wouldn't; and nothing is so nice to take, after a bad night, as coffee."

"How did you guess that I should not sleep?" enquired Romilly, as he proved his acquiescence in her sentiments by drinking her coffee.

"Because your friend is too boisterous, too *vif* for you," she replied without smiling. "I am glad he goes to-day; you will get well sooner without him, Monsieur. I am quite sure he has never had an aching head, he cannot know what it is."

"No! by Jove! nor an aching heart either," said Captain Romilly, sentimentally. "If you can cure one, Mademoiselle, perhaps you can cure the other."

"I know of an excellent remedy for either of them," replied Véronique demurely.

"Do you? what is that?" demanded the A.D.C.

"Silence, Monsieur!" she answered, placing her finger on her lip, but as she said so, Véronique laughed.

CHAPTER X.

A TOUCH OF THE GREEN-EYED MONSTER.

Captain Romer had rejoined his friends, and sent Romilly's belongings to him from the Avalanche Bungalow, by a native messenger, together with a brief note to say that he had brought down an ibex and a samba, "all by himself;" and that they should return to Ootacamund the following morning, where he hoped that the A.D.C. would soon be able to follow them.

But this event did not take place so soon as either of them anticipated. It was three days, notwithstanding the priest's liniments, before Captain Romilly could even leave his bed; three days before, with the aid of a stick, and Véronique's arm, he could hobble, laughing at his comical situation, yet groaning with pain the while, to the chair opposite Père Joseph's by the sitting-room fireside, and a couple more, before he could stand upright and walk like other men. The violent contusions he had incurred, left him for awhile, as stiff and helpless as though he had suffered from rheumatic fever; and he felt the effects of them for many a day after he had almost ceased to remember their existence. During this period of seclusion Véronique was constantly by his side, waiting on him as though she had been his servant, (for although his personal attendant had been sent with his clothes, Captain Romilly had a horror of being touched by a native, and shrunk visibly even from David's handling, a fact which the young man was not slow to observe;) and short as the time was, he had more opportunity during its course of reading the various phases of the girl's character, than months of ordinary acquaintanceship would have afforded him.

She was open as the day, but fitful as the channel waves; and every emotion which she experienced found immediate reflection in her countenance, which changed as many times in the twelve hours as the shadows of the sun. She was warm-hearted, and passionate as her Irish father: piquante and coquettish as her Belgian mother; but over all spread the influence of the pure country life she had led upon the Neilgherry hills, which neutralised much that might have been dangerous to her simplicity, and made that natural which would otherwise have been affected.

"Why do you always call me Mademoiselle?" she said on the second day of Captain Romilly's sojourn with them, as having performed some trifling office for him, she lingered by his bedside, plaiting her apron between her fingers, instead of leaving the room. "No one else does so, and it sounds so strange."

"But what else shall I call you?" he enquired,—"Miss Moore?"

"*Mon Dieu! non,*" with a merry laugh, "*ce serait encore plus drôle.*"

"What then?"

"Call me Véronique, Monsieur; I am known by no other name!"

"Very well, Mademoiselle; (Véronique, I mean,) I only waited for your permission. But then, you must promise on your part, no longer to call me Monsieur."

"I cannot speak your proper name," she said, shaking her head, "Rome-eely; it is too long and hard for me, Monsieur."

"But you must call me by my Christian name, Véronique."

"*Comment! Gor-don?*" she exclaimed, raising her dark eye-brows, "*c'est pire encore! cela me fendrait la bouche jusqu'aux oreilles.*"

He laughed at her dashing so suddenly into French; a certain sign with Véronique that she was becoming excited over her subject; and assured her that he would accept of no excuses, and that if he were to call her by her Christian name, she must learn to pronounce his. And so after a good many blushes and false starts, she made a compromise with her guest, and called him, "*Monsieur Gor-don,*" from that day.

But however pleased Véronique might be to wait upon the handsome aide-de-camp, and however assured Gordon Romilly of the welcome accorded him by both Père Joseph and his neice, there was one member of the priest's household who would have gladly contemplated his charms from a greater distance, and that was the young native David. An instinct, unrecognised by either man, had rendered these two antagonistic from the commencement of their acquaintance; and the more intimate Captain Romilly became with Véronique, the more did her adopted brother regard him with mingled dislike and fear.

"What has induced the Englishman to change his mode of addressing thee?" Romilly overheard him say one day, in French to Véronique. "Didst thou not run quick enough when he called thee

'Mademoiselle,' that now he must needs use thy baptismal name?"

"I know not," answered the girl carelessly. "What does it matter? one name is as good as another."

"Then, why dost thou call him, 'Monsieur Gor-don,' instead of plain 'Monsieur?' It is not the English custom, Véronique."

"I know nought about the custom," replied Véronique as she moved away from him; "Monsieur asked me to do so, *et cela m'est égal*," with which words Gordon Romilly heard her close the conference, by marching up to her own room.

He had suspected before that David was jealous of his intimacy with Véronique, and, now that he was sure of it, the discovery only made him anxious to cement the intimacy further. As the days went on, and the A.D.C.'s recovery progressed, the young native left no means untried—short of plain speaking—by which he might get rid of their guest. He suggested that a little wholesome exercise and change of air would expedite the cure; he volunteered to procure a " palanquin " and bearers from the cantonment, in which Captain Romilly might be carried back to Ootacamund; he even walked in there himself, and gave such an improved account of the A.D.C.'s condition to his friend Romer, that Romilly was immediately beset by notes of entreaty that he would make haste and rejoin them before they set out on their trip to Bandypoor. But all David's machinations to oust Captain Romilly from his position before he chose to quit it proved fruitless. He was too comfortable where he was, and too interested in his new acquaintances to have any intention of leaving them before he was absolutely obliged; and, secure of the smiles of Véronique, and the hospitable inclinations of her uncle, he could afford to laugh at poor David's jealousy, which he considered, both on account of his position and his blood, to be but another instance of his "d—d impertinence." But though the native appeared to make no secret of his feelings on the subject, they were evidently unsuspected by any one but his rival.

"Tell us something about Rêve, *mon père*," Véronique would say coaxingly of an evening, after Gordon Romilly had made his re-appearance in their family circle. "Relate to Monsieur Gor-don, how the good little sisters in the *maison réligieuse* used to dance and play about in the summer evenings with the children whom they taught; and how, when the sacrilege was committed at the cross-roads where the large crucifix stood, and some '*vilain*' robbed the box and threw the blessed cross upon the ground, the sisters rose two hours earlier every morning for a twelvemonth after, that they might restore, by their earnings for needlework, what the robbers had destroyed."

"*Quel idée!*" would David sarcastically utter from his corner, "as if Monsieur cared, Véronique, to hear what happened at Rêve fifty years ago. What interest can the childhood of *notre père* possess for him? Monsieur is not one of us!"

"*Tais-toi*," the girl would answer sharply in her turn, for she did not like rebuke, and took it least well when offered on any subject concerning Gordon Romilly; "what dost thou know of Monsieur Gor-don's likes or dislikes? Let Père Joseph judge for himself."

And then Captain Romilly would assure his host there was nothing he should like better than to hear some stories of the past; and the priest would look gratified, and Véronique triumphant; and David would retreat to the furthest end of the apartment and smoke his pipe in silent misery.

"I have very little to tell, Monsieur," Père Joseph would commence, "but if you should ever be near the spot, go to Rêve, and it will speak for itself. The bold hills swelling on either side of the valley—aye! bold as some of these, and densely clothed with vegetation—the bright river which glided like a serpent through the green fields, the tumbling water-falls spouting from the rocks, and the infinite variety of mosses, lichens, and ferns which peeped from every cleft, make Rêve in my remembrance an earthly paradise."

"It must have been beautiful," said Romilly, who had no more artistic taste for a fine view than he had consideration for David's feelings; but Véronique's eyes were sparkling at the description, and rewarded his affected enthusiasm with a glance of gratitude.

"Then the town," continued the priest, lost in a dream of the past—"I think as I sit here, Monsieur, that I can see the town, situated, as it was, upon a hill, with its one long, steep, irregular street, in which the houses of rich and poor, though placed side by side, still seemed to amalgamate, from being built of the same grey stone. My father's house stood in the centre of the street, behind a row of iron palings. It was always kept severely clean, that house. My mother would not allow a speck of dust to rest upon any part of her furniture, and the '*salon*' was forbidden ground to us children, even after we had attained to years of discretion. The '*parquet*' there was always so polished and so bright, the '*poêle*' such a miracle of shining blackness, and the embroidered white net curtains so spotlessly white, that I was even afraid to cross the room when summoned to it on state occasions, and used to leave my '*sabots*' in the hall outside."

"Bah! I should not like to wear '*sabots*,'" said Véronique, glancing at her dainty feet.

"Thou wouldst have been glad of them, had thou been born in Rêve," replied her uncle. "We never wore leather there except to mass, and when we went to be catechised by the priest."

"But tell of your visit to Brüssenburgh, *mon père;* when you went with your mother to see your father's family, and were taken to the greatest church in Belgium."

"Monsieur has doubtless been to Brüssenburg himself, and seen Ste. Geneviève, Véronique," was the priest's answer; "all are not such mountain cats as thou, remember!"

"Have you been there?" enquired the girl, with a look at Gordon Romilly.

"I have been at Brüssenburgh, Véronique, but I do not remember to have visited Ste. Geneviève."

"Then you missed a grand sight, Monsieur," Père Joseph replied; "as grand a sight as your St. Paul's, or Westminster Abbey. I think there is nothing makes a man feel so small, and so little contented with himself as to stand in one of those magnificent buildings, which are but bricks and mortar, and yet had their commencement ages before he began, and will stand, firm and unshaken, ages after he has crumbled into dust. Ste. Geneviève is a church to make one think thus, Monsieur. Of vast size, the light is admitted only through exquisitely-painted windows, each one of which is surrounded by a chapel, rich in *fresco*, carvings, and stone work, and dedicated to the tutelary saint. The altar and its surroundings are things to dream of; and the paintings, images, and other works of art with which the church is adorned, require a day's leisure to examine properly. You should have seen Ste. Geneviève!"

"I wish I had, and when I pass that way again I will not forget to visit it."

"But tell of thy seeing the king and queen in their carriage, *mon père*," said Véronique, who evidently considered that sight a far finer one than Ste. Geneviève; "and of the little prince who now sits upon the throne, riding about the park on his pony, in a hat and beautiful white feather!"

"Quiet, thou silly child!" replied Père Joseph, smiling. "Dost thou imagine that Monsieur thinks as much about a tuft of feathers as thyself? I tell such tales to thee because thou art no better than a baby; but Monsieur would think I took him for the same were I to repeat them now. Besides, he has been to Brüssenburgh, and doubtless seen the royal family for himself!"

"The present king I have," said Romilly, amused at Véronique's look of wondering incredulity at the news.

"Have you travelled much on the Continent, Monsieur?"

"Pretty well; but more in France and

Germany than Belgium. But when I return home I am very likely to go there again."

"And do you return to England soon?"

The question was put by the priest; but Véronique awaited the answer in breathless anxiety.

"I hope so! I intend to go as soon as ever I can."

"Monsieur does not like this country, then?"

"Not at all—in fact I hate it, and am doing all I can to get back to England again."

"Ah, well! For those who can afford it, home is the place to live in!" replied Père Joseph with a sigh; at which turn of the conversation, Véronique's face would considerably lengthen, and the eyes of David glisten with delight.

But Gordon Romilly had yet to be introduced to another phase of Véronique's character, neither grave nor gay, which, whilst it placed the girl in a new light before him, seemed to open his eyes to what he had half-hoped, and half-expected. It was on the fourth day of his stay at the priest's bungalow, when his back was so much better that Véronique had persuaded him to limp out into the sunny garden, and to sit on a chair against the palisades whilst she busied herself amongst her bees and blossoms.

"I never saw such a profusion of roses in my life before," he said, as he watched her pull flower after flower from the variegated hedge, and without causing any palpable difference in its appearance, "do they grow naturally, or have you cultivated them?"

"Almost naturally, Monsieur Gor-don," she answered, smiling, as she tossed a heap of white and pink beauties into his lap. "We set the plants in the first instance, of course, but they are never pruned, and they bloom from January until December. You have seen the garden hedges made of them in the cantonment, have you not?"

"Yes! but I thought they must be no end of trouble to keep up. But I find the sweetest things in this country, Véronique," he continued, with an expressive look in the girl's face, "are those which run most wild. The so-called cultivated part of the scenery, to say nothing of the so-called cultivated part of the community, is a great deal too tame for me."

She laughed softly and returned to her occupation. She did not half understand what Captain Romilly meant by his allusion, but she knew that he was paying a compliment to herself, and that was sufficient for her appreciation of it.

"Véronique!" he exclaimed, presently, "do come and look here! What is this long train of bullocks coming over the hills from the direction of Sispard? Men too, and, by Jove! women; who can they be?"

Véronique left her roses for a moment, and came and stood by Captain Romilly's chair, shading her eyes with her hand whilst she looked in the direction indicated.

"Those are 'Brinjaries,' Monsieur Gordon, and their cattle are laden with grain. They are passing here, on their way to Ootacamund, where they will probably part with most of the merchandise they carry."

"And what are 'Brinjaries,' Véronique? you forget what a griffin I am."

"Gipsies, Monsieur Gor-don, or something like it. They are wandering tribes whose chief wealth consists in cattle and grain: and they are always travelling about from place to place, disposing of, or exchanging it."

The long train of "Brinjaries" which, on account of the narrow pathway, was compelled to journey very slowly, now filed along the road at the bottom of the priest's garden, and as it passed, Captain Romilly observed that though most of the men made some kind of salutation to Véronique, the women never raised their eyes at all, but walked behind their lords and masters, handsomely clothed and covered with gold ornaments, but with looks strictly downcast, and hands meekly folded before them. This was on account of the " Brinjaries' " laws, which, regarding their women, are exceedingly stringent: so much so, that the least breach of chastity on their part, is immediately punished by death : a rule which makes the fair sex (and some of the "Brinjary" ladies are very fair) uncommonly well behaved.

"Look at the little children packed upon the bullocks, Monsieur Gor-don!" said Véronique, as a load of brown urchins of all shapes and sizes passed grinning before them. "Some of these 'Brinjaries' are said to be very rich, and really one would think so to see all the gold chains and bangles which they wear."

"Why do all the women hold their heads down?" demanded Romilly, "I haven't seen the face of a single one yet."

"They are not allowed to look about them!" said Véronique, quickly, "it is against their rules, and the men are very strict with them."

"What a shame," said Gordon Romilly. "I should like to catch one of the ladies without her blue beard husband, and see whether she would be so particular. By Jove, that must be a pretty girl!" he exclaimed, as he pointed out one that was just passing them, "what splendid hair she has, and what a beautiful figure. Just stand a little to one side, Véronique, I want to have another look at her!" and apparently forgetful of his stiff limbs, Captain Romilly jumped on the seat of his chair, and leant over the palisades to watch the retreating form of the "Brinjary" woman.

"Why, her hair is plaited with gold," he continued, "and what an immense length it must be, it hangs almost to her knees. Do you think it can be all her own? And what pretty little feet she has. I expect she must be a favourite wife, or, perhaps, a bride, for the fringe on her cloth is twice as deep as that of any other woman. I don't suppose she can be more than sixteen, or perhaps younger, eh, Véronique? I wish I could see her face."

Receiving no answer to his rhapsody, Captain Romilly turned to discover what had become of his companion, and to his astonishment, beheld her apparently busy at the other end of the garden, and quite beyond earshot of any of his remarks on the pretty " Brinjary."

" Véronique!" he exclaimed, "why, when did you run away ? I thought you were close beside me ;" and then he descended from his perch and found it a much more troublesome operation than the ascension had been. "Oh dear, oh dear! how my back does hurt me when I move. I really don't believe I'm any better to-day. What shall I do, Véronique, to make myself well ?"

"Take exercise, Monsieur; why don't you walk into the cantonment and back ?"

"You are laughing at me, Mademoiselle Véronique : you know I should be unable to accomplish that, unless, indeed, you would give me your arm for a support."

"There is not much chance of that, Monsieur."

"And why not? Are you quite tired of looking after me ?"

"I don't think you require any more looking after. You can jump on a chair so easily that your recovery must be nearly perfect."

"Have I offended you, Véronique?"

"Offended me, Monsieur?" with a little glance of haughty surprise. "*Mon Dieu!* how could you have offended me? You must not imagine every time I follow my household occupations that I have a cause for offence. When you were helpless I was glad to wait on you: now that you are so far recovered you will not mind sometimes waiting on yourself," and Véronique dug her spade vigorously into the flower-bed and turned the mould up, all over the A.D.C.'s feet.

Captain Romilly was in one of those dilemmas in which men who meddle with the "unfair" sex, occasionally find themselves, and for a little space he felt quite bewildered. He saw that something had occurred to annoy the girl before him, but what it was he could not for the life of him, imagine. He stood by her side for a few seconds, thoughtfully pulling his moustache, and wondering "why the deuce" women would be so unreasonable"; until seeing that one of Véronique's long tresses of hair had fallen over her shoulder in front and was impeding her vision, he ventured to touch it gently, with the intention of putting it back again. In a moment the girl's dark, blue eyes had flashed fire at him, and with a passionate gesture she seized the heavy plait from his hand, and flung it across her shoulder.

"*N'y touchez pas!*" she cried, indignantly, "*ma chevelure n'est pas assez longue pour vous plaire!*" and before Gordon Romilly could remonstrate with her petulance, or deny her words, she had burst into a flood of tears, and run away into the house to hide them. The circumstance flattered his conceit, already excited by her evident admiration of him, and he looked forward with anxiety to the moment when he should see her again. But Véronique did not re-appear until the evening meal was served, and then she bore no traces, either in looks or manner, of the emotion she had passed through. But Captain

Romilly could not help smiling to himself as he observed that, for the first time, she wore her luxuriant hair, (which, unplaited, reached considerably below her waist) loose about her shoulders, and the silent compliments thereon, which the A.D.C. paid her, with his eyes, signed a tacit peace between them, whilst it augmented the uneasy sensations of poor David.

But, on the following day, unable longer, either on account of his horse or himself, to extend with any decency his visit, Captain Romilly, to the secret gratification of the native, and the sincere regret of Père Joseph and his niece, returned to his quarters at the Ootacamund Hôtel.

CHAPTER XI.

THE OOTACAMUND POST-OFFICE.

Captain Romilly did not return to the cantonment in the very best of humours, either with himself or the world at large. In the first place he was vexed to think that he had injured his horse, a valuable animal, for which he had paid an exorbitant sum of money, extravagance being one of the most shining points in the luminous character of the A.D.C. It was true that the Arab was just able to limp back slowly to Ootacamund, but he promised to be unfit for active service for some time to come, and Captain Romilly did not relish the idea of mounting any meaner thing, and saw himself reduced in consequence to travelling about on foot. And he was vexed that he should have missed all the fun of the shooting excursion, to which he had looked forward with so much pleasure. He had pulled the trigger of his fine, new, double-barrelled gun, which, with its belongings, had cost him nearly a hundred pounds, about half-a-dozen times, and he had seen next to nothing of his old friend Romer— the only person on the hills of whom he had any knowledge, and whose company he should lose the following week. And above all this, Gordon Romilly was vexed that he was obliged to leave the priest's bungalow, without any reasonable excuse for revisiting it; and doubly vexed to think that he should be vexed to do so. Arrived at the Ootacamund Hotel, where he, as well as Captain Romer, was temporarily located, Romilly found that worthy in a great state of excitement, consequent upon his preparations for the shooting excursion to Bandypoor, on which he and Major Powell were to start the following day. He was most urgent in his entreaties that the A.D.C. should join them, and give them the enjoyment of his company for a couple of days further, but at first Gordon Romilly was sulky with his fate, and steadfastly refused; resolving to make himself as little pleasant as might be. But Romer's genial temper, added to a secret knowledge, on the part of the A.D.C., that the sooner he shook off the feeling which oppressed him, the better for himself, won the day, and from having felt inclined for nothing but to ride back to the priest's bungalow, and catch another glimpse of the smiling, pensive face of Véronique, Captain Romilly rushed into the other extreme, caught the infection of his friend's enthusiasm, bought a splendid Pegu pony from one of the native dealers, at his own price, and employed himself for the rest of the day cleaning, oiling, and arranging his weapons, whilst he discussed the merits of his new purchase, and expatiated on the feats of skill which he hoped to perform.

Meanwhile the figure of the little Irish girl grew dim in the background, and powder and shot, Pegu ponies, and Westley Richards' took its place. So much for the influence of the prettiest face in the world, when backed against a man's amusements with his own sex, in whatever direction they may happen to lie.

"Romilly! come up to the post-office with me," said Romer, on the following morning, for the A.D.C., having once got on his legs again, had made rapid progress, and, with the exception of a little stiffness, could now walk quite easily, "the mail is in, and we may as well see if there are any letters for us, before we start."

They set off at a smart pace in the direction Captain Romer indicated, and took their way through a rural lane, bordered by green hedges and overshadowed by leafy trees, along each side of which were gardens filled with summer flowers, and enclosing pretty rustic-built cottages, shaded by verandahs, and covered with creepers bearing orange and white and crimson blossoms.

"What a strange place this is!" said

Captain Romer, as he pointed out the beauties which they passed, "who would think, to look at those flower-beds, that the puddles were all ice at four o'clock this morning. Charmingly romantic, though, isn't it?—you must come here for your honeymoon, Romilly, if you ever have such a thing!"

"If I ever have such a thing," repeated the A.D.C., "I think I may promise you I will—but should I be so unfortunate as to be obliged to sell myself, Romer, I expect there will be more money than honey about the business, unless my present opinions materially alter."

"What nonsense! Surely, Romilly, you of all men, should be able to afford to do as you like in that particular!"

"If you think so, it only shows how little you can know of my affairs. I haven't got a sixpence of my own, Romer, and if you saw my cheque-book you'd be aware that his Lordship keeps me most uncommonly low."

"What do you call 'low?'" laughed

Romer, who had but his pay to depend upon, himself.

"Why! he only gives me five hundred a-year, beside my allowances, and it's impossible for a man to live decently on that. To say nothing of the unpleasantness of being always dependent on one's Governor —I can't move hand or foot without being hauled up for it!—it's 'Gordon this' and 'Gordon that,' and 'I'll stop your allowance, if I hear any more of it,' every month in the year!—Deuced unpleasant, you know! it gives your father such scope to take liberties with you. If it hadn't been for that, do you think I'd have come out to this country, and expatriated myself for a paltry A.D.C.ship, when I was quartered at Winchester, and could get up to Town every other night in the week? I would have seen myself further first! But that's the curse of being the youngest son —all three of my brothers are better off than myself, I wish they'd been at Jericho before they'd been born at all—but it's just like my luck; my mother ought to have been ashamed of herself." And as Gordon Romilly, with his youth and his beauty, his staff appointment, and his five hundred a-year, uttered this monody, he looked so truly pathetic, that Captain Romer burst out laughing.

"My dear fellow, it's a case for the consideration of your parish guardians, and you should not fail to place it before them as soon as ever you reach England again. Meanwhile, let us go and enquire for our letters."

"Which is the post-office?" asked Romilly, staring about him.

"That little building on the hill before you, next to the flag-staff."

"But what is that crowd of people collected round it?"

"Those are the residents of Ootacamund, waiting for their letters."

"Have you no postman, then, in this place?"

"Oh! yes! but they get their dispatches half an hour earlier by coming for them. They walk up to the post-office hill as regularly as the sun rises—it is something for them to do."

" Good Heavens !" exclaimed Romilly, as though lost in the contemplation of human nature sunk so low as to derive daily excitement from the contents of the postman's bag, " need we go inside ?"

" Oh! yes! you must see the Ootacamund Post-office ; for it's quite a curiosity in its way. I'll bet any money you never saw such another, wherever you may have travelled."

They could hardly force their way in for the assemblage of Europeans collected round the door, and amongst which might be seen specimens of almost every variety of the species then collected upon the Neilgherry Hills. Veterans, who had retired from the army to pass the remainder of their vegetable existence in that climate ; beardless " griffins," who had fallen sick on their first introduction to the country, and been hastily despatched upwards to prevent their being shovelled downwards ; officers, from Bengal, Bombay, and Madras, with yellow, parchment-like faces, who had undergone a wearisome course of "liver" and blue pills, and were trying what the sanatorium would do for them before they finally decided to take their "long leave home;" and soldiers from the various detachments stationed on the Hills, were all jostling one another in their efforts to get closer to a wire grating, which ran across one end of the inside of the post-office. The ladies of Ootacamund, also, were not unrepresented, although they did not show in such force as the men, but they made up for the deficiency of their number by the proficiency of their tongues, which kept up such a continual buzz, that when Romilly first found himself in the centre of the crowd, he could neither hear nor understand what it was all about.

"Try and edge your way towards the grating," whispered Romer in his ear; "the letters are all laid out on a counter behind it, and you will be able to see whether there are any for yourself, or not."

"All right!" said Romilly, "I will when

I find it possible to stir, but at present I am wedged in so tight that I can neither move one way, nor the other."

Meanwhile, the chatter and the buzz, intermingled with the gruffer tones of the male sex, went on incessantly. "Now, who can that letter for Mrs. Doveton be from, Miss Wheeler?—that one in the blue envelope, at the right-hand corner—I've never seen that hand before—a remarkable writing, too, hardly to be mistaken."

"I wonder if it can be young Arkwright's?" chimed in another voice, as the owner pushed forward to gain a sight of the suspected epistle, "it's really not unlike his writing. I'm almost sure that's the way he makes his D's! Just fancy if it is —how disgraceful!"

"Well, for my part I could believe anything in that quarter—particularly after the way in which she went on with him at the Rangalore Ball."

"Buffer has written to Bobson again," interposed a man's voice, "to ask him about the retirement money, I suppose, but it's of no use. Buffer will find that Bobson—"

But to what phase of Bobson's character Buffer had yet to be introduced, was lost in the medley of gratuitous news which was delivered on every side.

"But really, dear!" in a chirpy, harmless little tone, "if you'll promise *faithfully* not to repeat it, I'll tell you what I heard Mrs. ColonelDowdson say with her own lips about that business. She told me that—"

"Excuse me, my dear Mrs. Browne, it was nothing of the sort. She may *say* he proposed to her, but everyone knows—"

"Deny it? oh, nonsense! she *can't* deny it. Why he was seen coming out of the house!"

"Will you be good enough to make way here. I am in a hurry for my paper this morning! Yes, that one to your left! addressed Major Jones. Is not the next one for me?"

"No, sir; to the name of Steward."

"Steward—Steward! how very odd. I wonder who should send Steward papers!

All his friends are in England—frightfully in debt, you know. He'll never be able to leave the country."

"Ah, Major! it would be a good thing if his debts were the worst part of him. But that Rangoon business was quite shocking."

"*Low*, my dear! low is no name for her dress. I wonder that any gentleman liked to take her in to dinner. But I suppose that is the English fashion. and *we* know nothing."

"It will be a divorce, Miss Greene, and that before very long, mark my words!"

"Oh, dear! I hope not! so very scandalous, you know. But did I ever tell you what Mrs. Black said Miss White had told her she heard him say to her one evening at the Band? It was dreadful! She said that—" and here the fair coadjutors in promoting good-will amongst men, advanced their heads towards each other, and the thrilling climax which Gordon Romilly expected, was hissed into each other's ears.

"Oh! Mr. Graham," exclaimed a couple of ladies simultaneously, "here are three letters for you this morning, and one is in a lady's handwriting! Now, who is it from? You really must tell us. We are all anxiety to learn."

Mr. Graham, a young fellow of about Romilly's own age, pushed forward to the grating, seized his letters, and shoving them into his pocket with a growl that was half an oath, unceremoniously escaped from the pertinacious enquiries of his unlicensed persecutors.

"Always so rude!" exclaimed the ladies as they returned to the contemplation of the letters behind the grating, and then Captain Romilly who had recognised his father's splashy red seal from some little distance, heard them commence to speculate on the probable owner of the epistle.

"Captain, the Honourable Gordon Romilly, A.D.C.," said one as she nearly twisted her neck off, in her endeavours to read the address upside down; "I suppose that is one of the governor's *aides-de-camp*.

I didn't know there was anyone of that name upon the hills."

"It's a sweet name!" sighed a young lady who had been born and bred in her parents' adopted country.

"Colonel Thompson, do you know a Captain Romilly? we are so curious to know who he is."

"I have met a conceited young puppy who calls himself by that name," growled the Colonel, of whom nothing was to be seen except a huge, white, pith helmet, by which he was usually distinguished and extinguished when in the open air.

"Thank you!" said Gordon Romilly haughtily, some two inches above the white pith helmet, but the sound penetrating to the Colonel's ears, he looked up, got as red as a turkey-cock, and instantly disappeared in the crowd.

"My character precedes me!" remarked Romilly with a curl of his lip to Romer, but the ladies were too busy over the letter to have heard what had passed behind them.

"A lovely seal," quoth one, "and with a coronet on it! I wonder what that's for."

"Why, his father is a lord of course, and he'll be a lord himself by-and-bye, when his father dies."

"Will he? Are all honourables lords as soon as their fathers are dead?"

"*Of course* they are. Why, you silly thing! didn't you know that?"

The lady addressed, not liking to be thought so deficient in her knowledge of the customs and manners of the aristocracy, hastened to defend herself.

"Oh, yes! I was only joking. But fancy how nice! How I should like to see him! I wonder if he's tall."

Romilly's lip curled higher and higher as he listened to the remarks made upon himself, but he kept his patience wonderfully; and by dint of "I beg your pardon," and "will you allow me?" oft repeated, at last managed to approach the grating, near enough to speak to the official behind it.

"My letters, if you please?"

"What name?"

"Captain Romilly."

Romilly said the words as low as he could, but nothing escaped the ears of the idlers about the grating; and surprise occasioned by his unexpected appearance amongst them, caused such a general clustering and whispering together, that he and Romer experienced no difficulty in passing out of their midst again, and were soon clear of the post-office, and marching down the hill on which it stood.

"Well, thank heaven that's over," exclaimed Captain Romilly as they gained the open air; "I think I shall be content to wait for my epistles in future, until the postman brings them round. What a hotbed for idle talk and scandal that post-office appears to be. Why, most of those people had either received their letters or learnt that there were none for them, and yet there they stayed, blocking up the place just to chatter and gossip with each other. It only wanted cups of tea to be handed round to render the scene perfect."

"It is a *rendez-vous*," said Romer, in his

good-natured way of excusing everything, "and in this country people are so idle and so bored, that to look in each other's faces only is a relief. You will find just such another gathering in the market-place on Tuesdays and Fridays, Romilly."

"Excuse me, my dear fellow," replied the A.D.C., "I shall find no such thing, for I shall make a point, on the days you mention, of riding just in the opposite direction. If you have no wish to go further at present," he continued as he broke the seal of his letter and glanced over its contents, "I will ask you to walk back to the hotel with me, for this letter requires an answer, and perhaps I had better write it before we start."

"No bad news, I hope!" said Romer, with friendly anxiety.

"Well — not exactly, but my father's state of health is very unsatisfactory, and as I have not written to him for the last two mails, I am afraid he may think me negligent. Not that I am the favourite son by any manner of means, far from it, I am the prodigal and '*vaurien*' of the family; but the poor old governor's epistles, though crammed with good advice, are always kind, and I shouldn't like him to fancy himself neglected or forgotten."

Captain Romilly returned to the hotel, and wrote and dispatched his letter, and a few hours afterwards, finding himself mounted on the back of his stout Pegu, and making the descent of the " ghaut," with Powell and Romer, reverted to the scene he had witnessed at the Ootacamund Post-office, and expressed his opinion of it rather freely. Major Powell only shrugged his shoulders at the relation, as much as to say that it was a subject not worth arguing about; but Romer took up the cudgels in defence of it, and wielded them manfully.

"You are too hard upon them," he cried, "you forget the state to which a life of stagnation reduces people, bodies and minds, and should judge them by the standard of the habits of a little country village at home, and not by that of one of your bustling, go-a-head, thriving cities."

"Exactly so," replied Romilly; "but would they be pleased if you so judged them? To my mind they have every pretension to be considered as moving with the world, and are ready to be mortally offended with any one who appears to think otherwise. When I was down in Madras the other day, I met a man of some years' standing in the army, red-hot with passion over an article which had appeared in one of the magazines, reflecting on some of the customs and manners of the Anglo-Indians. He was perfectly furious about it. I thought the poor fellow would have broken a blood-vessel; but not being competent to judge whether the article in question were true or a libel, I could only express my sympathy with his outraged feelings, and remain silent. Well, would you believe it, the very same night at their mess-table, that man having recovered his spleen of the morning, was the foremost in relating a lot of stories (equivocal, to say nothing worse) of the ladies of that cantonment and others. I stared in amazement, and thought (what I have had occasion to think several times since), that if men in India are so touchy on the score of such things being remarked upon or repeated, why on earth are they the first to cram them down a stranger's throat? The land abounds with tittle-tattle and repetitions, and if what married men tell me is true, the women are not behindhand in spreading scandal of each other. One may talk, talk, talk in India as much as one likes, but directly it is whispered in England, or appears in print, the whole country is up in arms, at what has generally emanated from one of themselves."

"You speak the truth there," said Romer, gravely, "there is no doubt a vast amount of idle stories are constantly floating about; but you should remember that in so small a community as this, everything gets remarked upon. It is not that vice and folly are more prevalent with us here than they would be at home, but that they cannot be practised with such impunity."

"That may be the case," replied Romilly,

"though I am not prepared to implicitly avow it; but if it is, it does not alter the fact. During the few days we have spent in each other's company, you have told me yourself of half-a-dozen notorious cases, of which the subjects are still received in Indian society. I don't deny that these cases might have occurred in England, human nature being the same all the world over; but I do say that, had they been as openly discussed, the offenders would have been cut by all respectable people."

"But in a place like India, where you are brought into contact with your acquaintances every day, it would make one's position so unpleasant to be 'cuts' with half-a-dozen of them," said Romer.

"Then why make such a fuss about the matter? either be virtuously indignant, and shew your disapprobation of the proceeding, or—hold your tongue about it! But you Indians talk the greatest scandal of each other amongst yourselves; the names of men and women out here are handled with the most reckless impunity, (vide the conversation on the Post-office hill this morning!) and yet, if anyone else talks of you, you are surprised where they could have gained their information."

"No one likes being abused, of course," observed Captain Romer.

"Then why abuse each other? I never heard any Madras scandal in England, though I have been told that to listen to a lot of old Indians at Bath or Brighton, who have met together to talk over their reminiscences, is a caution, and beats all the books in their disfavour that were ever penned. But I have not been so fortunate. I received my information from your own mouths when I arrived in this country, where, you may depend upon it, Indian scandal always has its rise. Madras is like the adder who stings herself to death."

"And what of Bengal and Bombay?" said Romer, laughing.

"Oh! I know nothing of the sister Presidencies," returned Gordon Romilly, in the same strain; "but if what one hears of Simla and other places, is true, they have all three rightly earned their title to be considered feminine. For though want of something to talk about may make men descend to repeating stories, injurious to the characters of their friends, you may take your affidavit, Romer, that it is the women who provide them with the means. We may promulgate a scandal, but it is they who originate it."

"Hear! hear! hear!" exclaimed Romer, sitting well back on his saddle, and sticking out his legs straight before him. "A Romilly come to judgment! Why, my dear fellow, you are quite a moralist! You must lecture on the subject as soon as you get back to Madras, and I'm sure all the ladies will flock to hear you, if only on account of the fascination attached to your name."

"I daresay they would," said the A.D.C., carelessly; "but I don't intend to honour them. You may laugh at my arguments, Romer, as much as ever you like, but as long as you listen, and have nothing wherewith to answer me, I feel perfectly satisfied both with them and myself."

And as Captain Romilly, bestriding his handsome Pegu, blew a thin curling cloud of smoke into the air from between his supercilious lips, he looked as though his words were true.

CHAPTER XII.

"ERIN" AMONGST THE TODAHS.

THE two days' shooting at Bandypoor was a perfect success. No further *contretemps* happened, to ruffle the serenity of the A.D.C., or to mar the pleasure of his friends; and it was a time to be remembered by all of them with satisfaction. As for Captain Romilly, he was almost ready at the close of it to admit that under some circumstances life might be enjoyable even in the East, though Romer took care not to risk the disturbance of his companion's new-born contentment, by suggesting so treasonable an idea to him. He had brought down to his own gun two spotted deer, one tiger-cat, and at least a dozen and a half rose-necked parrots, to say nothing of having mortally alarmed a baby elephant, which he had caught attempting to browse on the outskirts of the jungle, and which, after having sent a bullet whizzing close to its tender trunk, he had caused to beat a hasty retreat to the side of its dam, to the tune of its own shrill trumpeting of fear.

So divinely affable, however, was the temper of the Honourable Gordon during these few days of sequestration, that he would not permit even this disappointment to elicit more than a naughty word from him; and consoled himself by having his deer-skins stretched and dried, preparatory to being transformed into half-a-dozen pairs of slippers, and making his rose-necked parrots into a pie, which he vowed was the best which he had ever eaten.

Their sport at Bandypoor was decidedly ordinary; but the cheerfulness and *verve* which all three men threw into the undertaking, caused the holiday to be a very pleasant one; and when at the close of the third day, Gordon Romilly shook hands with Powell and Romer for the last time, and mounted his stout little pony to re-ascend the "ghaut" by himself, he felt lonelier and more dispirited than he could have believed it possible he should be.

"Good-bye! old chum," was Romer's farewell advice, "get a jolly wife as soon as you can, and see if she won't reconcile you to staying in India sooner than anything else would do!"

"A wife! my dear fellow. You might as well advise me to try hanging in order to make me contented with life. You are a great deal more likely to put your head in the noose than I am."

"I wish I could," said Romer with a shrug. "I'd try it fast enough, Romilly, if I had the means, for it's the best thing a man can do after all."

"*Chacun à son gout*," was the unsympathetic rejoinder. "With me, Romer, the charms of married life, like those of India, gain in proportion to the less I see of them —'Distance lends enchantment to the view.'"

"You don't deserve to see it any nearer,"

replied the other jestingly, and his merry laugh was the last thing that Gordon Romilly heard as he turned his pony's head in the direction of the "ghaut."

As he ascended it, he hardly observed its order of high romantic beauty, which could not but have been appreciated, even by his inartistic eye, had his mind not been full of another subject. But he felt quite "hipped" at the prospect of returning to Ootacamund without the genial presence of Romer, who was not only the sole person he had liked there, but the sole person he had known. He had applied for leave to the hills, hardly aware of what he should do or find there; and his *rencontre* with his old schoolfellow had been one of those happy accidents which we occasionally experience through life, and for which we are not sufficiently grateful. But his meeting Captain Romer, with whom he had been intimate in days gone by, and speaking his mind so freely to him in consequence as he had done, had been the means of making him more enemies than friends amongst those who had been the recipients of his opinions; and Romilly knew that, without the shield of Romer's companionship he should find a difficulty in mixing on anything like terms of intimacy amongst those whom he had offended. He told himself, as he performed the slow and fatiguing ascension of the "ghaut," that the fact could make no possible difference to him, that he had nothing in common with the residents of Ootacamund, nor they with him; and that familiar intercourse between them would be productive of neither pleasure nor profit on either side.

Notwithstanding which private assertion, Captain Romilly was not such a fool as to be unaware that, as we journey through this world, we are all dependent upon one another for comfort and enjoyment; and he remembered that he was a greater stranger here than he had been even in Madras; and felt proportionately friendless and alone.

But as he ruminated on these things, the thought of Père Joseph and his niece flashed across his mind, and Romilly's breast positively glowed as he recalled the hospitality which had been shown him from that quarter, the cordial welcome with which he had been received, and the honest regret which had followed his departure. He had almost forgotten the Roman Catholic priest and his family, amidst the pleasures of his shooting excursion; but now the recollection of them and all their kindness, diverted his thoughts into a pleasanter channel as he commenced to consider by what means he could best express his sense of all they had done for him during his late visit to the bungalow.

The A.D.C. was very extravagant, but he was generous at the same time, and his money was far oftener spent on others than on himself. From the first hour that he had been laid on the priest's bed, he had intended to remunerate him handsomely for his trouble; but at the same time it was difficult to know in what way to do it, for an offer of money he felt that Père Joseph would reject with scorn. Had he been in England or France, he would have sent him the works of Victor Hugo, Blaise Pascal, or Chateaubriand, for the priest was a well-educated man, as his conversation denoted, and the want of books in his own language was one of the few privations at which he had murmured in the presence of his guest. But whilst making a note to have a box of literary food sent out for him from England as soon as possible, Captain Romilly did not wish to defer making Père Joseph some little offering until they arrived, and for a long time he could not imagine what sort of article would be most acceptable to the old man. At last he thought of an easy chair, for the sole one of which the little bungalow could boast was old-fashioned and worn; and so elated was he at his own ingenuity, that as soon as he reached the cantonment he could not rest until he had ransacked the stores of English furniture in the native shops, and found the article which he desired. A very handsome chair it was too, with a mahogany frame, covered in morocco; such an one as the priest's bungalow had never known even in its palmiest days; and a handsome price did Mr. Hubbubbetty

Chetty charge the unsuspecting A.D.C. for it, but who would have paid the sum twice over sooner than not have had what he had set his heart on procuring.

The same evening it was dispatched, by the hands of two coolies, to its destination, accompanied by a very pretty little note of thanks. And that it gave great pleasure there, and doubtless excited universal admiration, was proved by the answer, which, written in French, and in the crabbed foreign hand of Père Joseph, reached Gordon Romilly on the following morning—

"Monsieur—

"I have received, with the greatest pleasure, the magnificent present which you have had the kindness to send me. I cannot better express my gratitude for your remembrance of me, than by saying, that during my life I shall guard it with the greatest care; and after my death I shall leave it to my child, as a *souvenir* of the brave and generous Englishman who honoured us by staying under our roof. In conclusion, may I hope, that it will not be many days before your goodness gives me the opportunity of saying in person what I find it difficult to write. Receive, Monsieur, the assurance of my most perfect consideration.

"JOSEPH QUETIN."

When Captain Romilly read this note, which vividly recalled the memory of the frank cordiality with which the courteous old priest had received him, he was immediately seized with an unconquerable longing to rush out to the bungalow, and see Père Joseph and Véronique again.

This feeling, which had assailed him strongly ever since he had re-entered the cantonment and missed the companionship of his friend Romer, was but natural under the circumstances, but Captain Romilly knew sufficient of his own disposition to be aware that it was dangerous for him. He had felt interested in the little Irish girl from the first day that he had seen her, and when, recovered from his accident, he had left her uncle's house, the knowledge that he did not like to part from Véronique had been the cause of his very palpable ill-humour.

She was attractive from every point of view, pretty enough to satisfy the demands of any man : educated enough to make him totally forget the difference in her station, and *piquante*, and coquettish enough to drive him to do anything foolish in order to see her at his feet. A dangerous companion for any one who did not intend to make her his wife, and particularly so for a man with the peculiar temperament of Captain Romilly. For when he had told Romer, on the first occasion of their meeting, that he had never cared for a woman, and never expected to do so, the A.D.C. had not adhered strictly to the truth. He had certainly never yet felt what it was to conceive a pure, faithful love for one individual, and to cleave to it ; but as for what is termed " falling in love,"—that is, generating a hot fancy for a pretty face, not to be cured until a prettier comes in view,—Gordon

Romilly had been doing scarcely anything else, ever since he had arrived at years of indiscretion. It was on this account, and because he had become entangled with society beneath himself in point of station, that his father, Lord Erskine Romilly, had procured him his present appointment of aide-de-camp, and insisted upon his accepting it. He was truly as he had remarked to Romer, the prodigal and *vaurien* of his family, and the problem which his relations were constantly trying to solve for themselves, was: what would eventually become of "poor Gordon." Meanwhile "poor Gordon," spoilt by women on account of his face, and tolerated at the least, by men, on account of his birth and position, had not yet commenced (except on the score of his supposed poverty) to consider himself an object for universal compassion. Notwithstanding all his affectation of finding his existence a bore too great to be endured, he knew that his life was passing very pleasantly away, and he was not a person who concerned himself about the future.

To-day was the god of Gordon Romilly, he let to-morrow take care of itself.

Now, when he felt that his interest in Véronique Moore was becoming deeper than it should be, he ought, knowing how quickly his fancy was apt to be entangled, to have turned his steps away from that part of the hills altogether, and sought a refuge from himself in Coonoor, or Jackatella.

We ought all to do the wise and prudent thing when temptation, like an armed man, meets us in the way; only, unfortunately for the credit of our powers of fighting, nine hundred and ninety-nine out of a thousand, prefer standing their ground and doing warfare for themselves. And though the pathway be strewn with the bodies of the slain, and the air resounds with the cries of the fallen, it would seem as though human nature were too proud to fly from the devil, though it knows that a hand-to-hand combat invariably ends in its defeat.

Gordon Romilly knew that he had no intention of wooing Véronique Moore to be his wife, such an idea had never entered his head, still less had he any design of injuring her. Perhaps he was not quite clear at that moment, what he did mean, but he knew that he liked to make love to a pretty girl, and to have his already sufficiently good opinion of himself bettered, by seeing how his attentions fluttered and excited her. And, therefore, as the prospect of that pleasure lay bright and shining in the path before him to-day, he pursued it as a thoughtless child pursues a painted butterfly, although the insect, in attempting to elude his grasp, may lead him over a precipice. He very much wished to make some little gift to Véronique as well as to her uncle, but had not thought of anything which appeared to him suitable to her position, until, in turning over the contents of one of his portmanteaux after his return to Ootacamund, he lighted upon a small jeweller's box containing a sapphire ring which he had purchased in Madras. He had not bought the trinket, which was composed of remarkably fine stones, with the view of giving it to any particular person: for, thoughtless as he was extravagant, costly articles constantly found their way into his possession, simply because he admired, or considered them cheap at the price.

Now, however, as he caught sight of the ring with its brilliant blue stones, and thought how Véronique's eyes would sparkle as he placed it on her finger, regardless of the value and inappropriateness of the gift, he put the box into his pocket, resolved to give it to her the next time they met; and when, on the receipt of Père Joseph's note, he ordered his Pegu to the door, and rode away without an attendant, in the direction of the priest's bungalow, he had it still about him.

The morning was exquisitely clear, and the atmosphere was soft and balmy—the sun had not yet climbed the highest heaven, and his warmth, without being oppressive, was just sufficient to draw forth the scent of the thousand and one flowers which blossomed in the cantonment, and made the air luscious with their fragrance. The carriage-road, about the lake, was full of moving figures; "tonjons," bearing heavy weights, and being borne by groaning bearers, men and women mounted on horseback, "bullock-bandies," full of children, rocking like boats at sea, from the ungainly movements of the awkward beasts that drew them, and open and shut vehicles of all sizes and descriptions, made the place look unusually lively.

And through them all rode Gordon Romilly, looking, for him, unusually lively also. The complaining grunting chant of the "tonjon" bearers did not appear to disgust him as it was wont to do; the sight of the bullock-drivers urging on their unfortunate animals by means of twisting round their tails and pricking them with an iron pointed goad, no longer provoked him to a shudder; he was tolerant of the glances shot at him by some of the "really not bad-looking" pairs of eyes which he encountered on his way, and even returned the broad grins with which the black "ayahs," robed in their red and white cloths, saluted him in passing.

He felt, for once, light-hearted and content, but did not choose to recognise, or would not stay to enquire the reason of the change within him, although, more than once before, he had plunged into the intoxicating waters, on the brink of which he stood, and which have the power to alter the face of all external things for those who live in them.

He might have guessed it, when he had left the Cantonment behind him, and felt how fast his heart beat at the thought that each step brought him nearer to the bungalow beside the little chapel. Yet he went on, doggedly determined not to acknowledge to himself how very much pleasure the anticipation of this visit gave him, but humming a tune, nevertheless, as he beat time with his Malacca cane on the "hogged" mane of his dauntless Pegu.

He was within a quarter of a mile of the residence of Père Joseph, and still sunk in a kind of dreamy reverie, when he was startled by hearing a voice call, "Monsieur!" some way below him, and looking down the side of the hill which he traversed, he perceived the slight figure of Véronique scrambling up the acclivity towards him. With the small uncovered head, the long hooded cloak, and the large gold ear-rings, it was unmistakably herself, and the suddenness of the *rencontre* sent Romilly's blood flying so fast through his veins, that by the time she had reached the side of his pony, her face flushed with the speed she had exercised, his cheeks were almost as glowing as her own.

"*Ah! Monsieur! vous pouvez monter à cheval, vous vous portez mieux, j'en suis bien aise,*" poured from her voluble little lips, and then she stood, blushing and agitated beside him, and looking as though she had done wrong in attracting his attention.

"What a pretty pony!" she added, to cover her confusion, as she laid her hand upon the Pegu's bristling mane.

Gordon Romilly seized it.

"I was on my way to see you, Véronique —that is to see Père Joseph. Is he not at home?"

"No, Monsieur," gently withdrawing her hand, "I am sorry to say he is not—and David, he also is away. There is no one in the bungalow; I locked the door, and hid the key behind the beehives, but if you would like to go on, and rest, you can open the door for yourself, and they will both be home to dinner. *Mon père* will be so pleased to see you, Monsieur! Ah! what a beautiful chair that is you sent him; and how good of you to keep him in your thoughts—too good! we all thank you much, Monsieur."

"And where are you going, Véronique?" enquired Captain Romilly, professing to ignore her grateful glances, "I don't anticipate paying a visit to an empty bungalow."

"I am going in search of my little cow, Monsieur—she is such a naughty little thing, is 'Erin;' if ever she can stray away, she does, and yesterday she left the buffaloes to come home by themselves. But

I think she has wandered after the Todahs' cattle, for she has been there two or three times before, so I am going to their village to enquire."

"'Erin' amongst the Todahs!" laughed Romilly, "that is quite a new idea, Véronique! And how far off may the Todahs live?"

"About half a mile from here, Monsieur."

"And mayn't I go with you?"

The girl looked uneasy.

"You could not ride, Monsieur; my way lies right across the hills, and it will be too steep for your pony."

"But I can lead him, Véronique; I should not think of riding whilst you were on foot."

"I shall not go over any beaten path, Monsieur, and those Pegus are sometimes very obstinate when led; he might refuse to follow, and break his rein, or pull you backwards."

"Then I shall let him go by himself. Come, Véronique, it is of no use making objections to my company, because I am quite determined to look for 'Erin,' with you, in the Todahs' village—I have never seen a Todah yet, and you promised once that you would show me one."

"Very well, Monsieur, do as you please," replied the girl, with a slight sigh, as she waited until Gordon Romilly had dismounted and thrown his pony's bridle across his arm, before she led the way in the direction where the straying "Erin" was supposed to be.

CHAPTER XIII.

MONSIEUR! JE NE PEUX PAS.

As Captain Romilly rode on his way to the priest's bungalow, he had thought of a hundred different things which he intended to say to Véronique, but strange to relate, when he found himself alone with her upon those solitary hills, so far removed from the habitation or the cognisance of man, that he might have said or done what he had chosen with impunity, his eloquence failed him, and he walked by her side in silence. This difference was partly owing to the manner of the girl herself, which, from being all excitement and pleasure at meeting him again, had changed, most unaccountably, to a shy reserve; and partly to his own feelings, which proved stronger than he had given them credit for. They paced beside each other for more than five minutes, without speaking a word, and then Véronique, who could bear the silence no longer, said abruptly :

"You are better, Monsieur, quite well, are you not?"

"Yes! I think I may pronounce myself quite well again, Véronique, at least as far as my bruises are concerned," and with that he stole a side glance at her, to see if she had noticed the insinuation, but perceiving no signs of it, twitched the Pegu's bridle violently instead, and desired him to "keep up."

"*Le bon Saint Hubert* has not forgotten you," said the girl, thoughtfully. "Have you been reading or thinking anything about him since we parted, Monsieur?"

"Monsieur," who had almost forgotten the pre-existence of Saint Hubert at all, here stammered out that he had been prevented doing what was so greatly his desire, by the shooting excursion to Bandypoor, which necessarily usurped much of his time. But Véronique did not seem to notice that he was confused.

"*Mon père* has told me," she answered, "that Saint Hubert is the patron saint of the chase, therefore Monsieur could hardly have a more appropriate guardian. He was very wicked at one time, was Saint Hubert, and he used to hunt on Sundays, which is very wrong, of course. You never do so, Monsieur, do you?" with an appealing look, which at the same time was rather doubtful, until Romilly had assured her that he never did.

"He was out hunting one Sunday, as usual," continued the girl, " in the great forest of the Ardennes, when a beautiful stag ran across the path, and as he raised his bow to shoot at it, it turned to face him, and there was the crucifix just between its horns. Saint Hubert was not a saint at that time, you understand, Monsieur, but when he saw this blessed miracle, he fell on his knees, and was converted at once; and he built a church on the very spot, and founded a monastery in the town, into which he retired till his death."

"And never shot a stag on Sunday again," said Romilly, laughing, "what a good boy."

But Véronique's quick look of distress and horror recalled him to a sense of the profanity of which he had been guilty.

"Monsieur, Monsieur! you cannot be thinking of what you say!"

"I beg your pardon, Véronique!" he answered, sobered in an instant; "but, really, do you mean to tell me you believe that story?"

"Of course I do, Monsieur! am I not a Catholic? and are we not bound to accept the traditions of the Church? Surely you believe it also."

Upon this appeal, sundry recollections of the Council of Trent, and the requirements of the Roman Catholic religion flitted in an undefined manner through Gordon Romilly's brain, but it was all misty to him, and he felt sorry for the first time, that he had, however unwittingly, deceived the innocent child beside him, who was looking so earnestly in his face for a denial of what she feared.

He longed to tell her then, that she was mistaken in him, and that he was a Protestant who had abjured all such Popish errors; but he felt that the avowal would make her shrink from, and perhaps distrust him ever afterwards, and he had not the courage to confess his faith. So he answered vaguely—

"Well, you see I'm such a sinner, Véronique, that it is hard for me to believe in such things. But tell me what became of my patron Saint—I ought to know."

"He lived in the monastery till he died, Monsieur, and then he was buried in the church. Père Joseph has seen his tomb; for the town Saint Hubert, which was named after him, is only a few leagues distant from Rêve. Perhaps if you saw his tomb, you would also believe."

"Oh! I believe all right enough, Véronique! don't be afraid of that! but I want to know what I have done that I am to be nothing but Monsieur with you again! You promised to call me by my own name, if I used yours, and yet I have been gone but five days, and you have already forgotten it—how is that?"

"*Je ne l'ai pas oublié,*" she said, softly.

"Then why don't you use it? Has it altogether too rough and barbarous a sound for your dear little mouth?" and as Captain Romilly put the question, he placed his disengaged arm about her slender waist.

Véronique did not object, or twist herself away, but she grew very crimson, and the tears welled slowly into her downcast eyes.

"Won't you say it, Véronique? it sounds sweeter from your lips than I ever heard it sound before."

"*Oh! Monsieur, je ne dois pas, je ne peux pas.*"

"And why not?"

He was becoming so used to hear her express herself in French whenever she was agitated, either pleasantly or otherwise, that he took no notice of the change, but continued the patchwork conversation as composedly as though it had all been in the same language.

"Why not, Véronique? has anyone been setting you against me, or trying to make you believe that we are too intimate?" a thought of David and his jealousy flashing across him.

But she shook her head.

"Then perhaps you have ceased to regard me as a friend of your own accord. I am not so sincere or so honest as you expected. I have disappointed you in some way, and you already regret that you have shown me so much kindness. Is it so?"

"Oh! Monsieur, pray do not say such words."

"Then you must tell me what has altered you, Véronique."

But at that moment they came in sight of the Todahs' "maunds."

"There is the village!" she said quickly, "pray, Monsieur, take away your arm. Père Joseph would be angry were we seen thus."

He withdrew his arm at once, and walked

apart from her a little sulkily. He could not understand why she should repulse his advances, who but the other day had seemed so ready to attract them. The Todahs' village, called so for want of a better designation, was simply a collection of "maunds," as their dwellings are termed, heaped together like so many ant-hills. They were not unlike ant-hills, either, except in point of size, being long, low habitations formed of red earth, with rounded sides, and apertures for entrance so small that the Todah men were compelled to go on all fours in order to enter their houses, and Gordon Romilly was at a loss to imagine how the ladies (in general much broader and bulkier than their lords), managed to get in or out at all.

There seemed to be very little life moving about the Todah village when they first approached it, for the men were away, herding the droves of buffaloes, in which their wealth consists, and of children they saw none; but presently, a woman, attracted by the sound of their voices, appeared on all fours, at the entrance of her "maund," and, showing her white teeth, in sign of welcome, dragged herself into the open air, and stood upon her feet.

"Did you ever see such dreadful places to live in?" timidly enquired Véronique of Captain Romilly, who had not addressed her since she had last spoken to him, "these 'maunds' are so filthy and so dark inside, that I have heard Père Joseph say that when the commonest coolies are overtaken by a storm upon the hills, they prefer to lie out in the soaking rain to entering one of the Todahs' huts; they are so full of fleas and other vermin."

"From the look of them I am not surprised to hear it," answered Romilly.

The woman who now approached them, was a fine specimen of her race, being tall and well-formed. Her hair, in rich dark curls, hung down to her waist; her features were good, though coarsely moulded, and the blanket, which, pinned at her throat, was the sole covering she wore, revealed an arm and leg according with the rest of her person.

She grinned vehemently as she exchanged a few words with Véronique on the subject of the lost cow, and pointing to a rough shed, a little distance off, intimated that "Erin" was there, and that she would go and fetch her.

"They have my cow," said Véronique, as the Todah woman walked away, "I thought that I should find her here. Do you know, Monsieur, that that woman who has just left us, has sixteen husbands."

"By Jove!" exclaimed the startled A.D.C.

"She has, indeed! and some have even more. By their laws, when a girl is once married, if another man desires her for his wife, he has to make his proposals to the first husband, and it depends upon how many buffaloes he possesses, whether he is accepted or not; then the third one has to obtain the permission of both the other husbands; and so on. They all put their buffaloes together, so, of course, the more there are the richer they become; but it is a very strange custom, is it not?"

"Devilish strange!" responded Captain Romilly.

"The men spend all their time in looking after the cattle, and the wives stay at home and cook the dinners in these dreadful huts. Oh! here are two more women coming to speak to us; and see, Monsieur, they are bringing a baby to show you."

"A baby!" exclaimed Romilly, in horror, "I wish they wouldn't! I've a perfect detestation of them."

The Todahs were close to them by this time, and in their arms they held up a little fat child, with glittering black eyes, and a head covered with tufts of curling hair, for the inspection of the strangers.

"It is a great curiosity," said Véronique, smiling, "or they think it so, Monsieur. This is the only baby in the village, and the first that has been born here for the last four years. *Mon père* says that the Todah race is completely dying out."

"So much the better for them and for us, I should think," said Romilly, grimly, as he kept edging to one side and the other, in order to avoid the too near approach of the dreaded baby ; until, at the suggestion of his companion, he threw the mother a piece of money, and she retired, with her treasure, to her " maund."

The little cow now made its appearance, led by a halter, and Véronique, after rewarding its finder according to her means, threw the rope across her arm, and prepared to conduct her favourite back to its home.

Whilst they had been detained in the Todah village, she had spoken fast and continuously to the A.D.C., in order to cover the annoyance which the last words exchanged between them had caused her, but now that they were once more alone, she felt as though all her courage had evaporated, and laying her head gently against the neck of the truant " Erin," pretended to be reproaching her for her misdeeds, whilst, in reality, she was struggling to keep back the tears which threatened to overflow her eyes.

"Happy ' Erin,'" said Gordon Romilly,

as he remarked the action, " your mistress extends to you the welcome which evidently she has not got for her friend."

" Monsieur, you should not speak like that !" replied Véronique, as she lifted her face from the cow's neck, and let him see how weary it appeared.

" Then what is between us, Veronique ? why do you refuse to call me ' Gordon ?' Why did you object to my accompanying you hither ?"

She was again silent, and taking the sapphire ring from its case, he held it towards her, saying—

" See ! what I had brought you, in hopes that you would accept it, in remembrance of all the kindness with which you tended me whilst I was ill."

She glanced up at the sparkling jewel, and had half-uttered an exclamation of natural admiration, but the next moment her voice and eyes fell, and she resumed her former melancholy look.

" I shall never forget those days, Véronique," continued Gordon Romilly, " nor how carefully you tended me; and I had thought that you also might look back upon them with something not unlike pleasure."

He gazed into her face as he spoke, and saw that tears were falling on her cloak. The sight encouraged him.

"My dear Véronique! I am sure that you are only playing with me; your tears deny your words—I cannot have been utterly mistaken when I fancied that you liked me, just a little bit—was it not true?"

He was bending down, and almost whispered in her ear, and as he did so he caught a murmured "*oui*."

"Then let me put this ring upon your finger, Véronique, and wear it there, in token that we are friends, and shall continue so."

But Véronique drew backward, and would not let him even take her hand.

"*Non, Monsieur, ne me le demandez pas, je ne le puis pas, vraiment! je ne le puis pas.*"

"And why not?" he demanded almost angrily, "has Père Joseph forbidden you? has that fellow David dared to influence you? why will you not take my gift, Véronique? I must have an explanation."

Frightened by his vehemence, she turned with terrified eyes and trembling lips to cling to his arm.

"*Mon Dieu! ne m'effrayez pas ainsi, et je vous dirai tout.*"

"No one has spoken to me of you, Monsieur," she resumed after a short pause, during which she was trying to steady her voice, "what I think and feel has all come from myself, from my heart here," laying her hand upon her breast, "I liked to nurse you, Monsieur Gor-don, I liked also to have you for my friend, and you saw that I liked it. But after you were departed, I questioned with myself whether to like you so much was good or safe for me! and I could not but answer no! It would be very pleasant, doubtless, whilst it lasted, but soon you will be gone, and I shall have no friend, and then, what is to become of me? For the same reason, Monsieur Gor-don, I will not take your ring; it is like your friendship, too valuable, too fine, for my poor life. It does not accord with it, I am better without the ring—or you!"

He felt the truth of her objections to his heart's core, although they did not please him, and he walked beside her silently, with his eyes bent on the ground, as he pulled his long fair moustaches through his fingers, and considered in what words to answer her.

"*N'ai-je pas raison?*" she whispered, presently, but the reply was dubious.

"Yes! I suppose you are right, Véronique, though it's a deucedly unpleasant prospect to contemplate."

"But it must be wrong to amuse ourselves," she urged, casting a timid glance at the tall figure beside her, "when so much harm might come from it."

"And suppose the harm has come already," said Romilly, rashly, "suppose I have a deeper interest in you than that of friendship, Véronique, what then?"

A flush of glad surprise spread itself over the girl's brow and bosom, and for an instant she had almost yielded to the intoxication of the discovery, and confessed that the feeling was mutual; but the next moment, (recalling the difference in their positions) the hot blood retreated as suddenly as it had come, and left her sick and trembling with the bitter disappointment.

"Monsieur, that would be worse than all. You must not even speak of such a thing!"

"Worse than all," repeated the A.D.C., as he put his arm again about her supple waist, "how dreadful a calamity my love must seem to you, Véronique."

He saw the tender light which stole into her soft eyes at the thought, and emboldened by it, bent his lips towards hers. But before he could reach them, Véronique had placed her hand upon her mouth, and disengaged her slight form from his grasp.

"*Non non! vous ne devez pas faire cela!* you must not do that," she exclaimed loudly, in her excitement, "for what do you take me, Monsieur? You ask for my love, for my embraces, and you will give me in return — what?"

"*My* love, darling," said Captain Romilly, who was growing more eager the more he was repulsed, "isn't that a fair exchange?"

"And how will your love end, Monsieur?" asked the girl, still keeping aloof from her companion.

At this point-blank question, put with fearless eyes, the face of the young man fell, and Véronique perceived it. The flush which excitement had raised upon her cheeks, faded slowly away; and dropping her disengaged hand listlessly by her side, she hid her face against the dappled neck of "Erin" and burst into tears.

"Don't cry, Véronique, pray don't cry," urged the A.D.C., ruefully, "I am an awful fool to have said anything about it." But that was all the consolation he could find it in his heart to give her.

"You see, Monsieur," said Véronique, after a while, as she wiped the traces of grief from her countenance, "that I am right, and that anything beyond the commonest acquaintance between us, is quite out of the question. You are a gentleman, above me in birth, and station, and everything, and I am only a poor country girl, the daughter of a soldier, and unfit in every way to be your companion. Were you to meet with another accident, I should be as glad to nurse you as I was before, and whenever you can spare time to ride out to our bungalow, no one will be more pleased to see you than myself. But there, let it rest, Monsieur, never speak to me again, as you have done to-day, nor offer me souvenirs of this time; for it is best that I should forget it—and you also."

"I wish to heaven we had never met!" exclaimed the young man passionately.

"And so do I, Monsieur," was the simple reply, and then they walked the rest of the way in silence, their hearts within them burning, the one with disappointed passion, the other with pure regret.

"Well, good-bye, Véronique," said Gordon Romilly, as they again reached the spot where he had met her, "I don't feel inclined to go on to the bungalow to-day, but you can tell Père Joseph that you met me, and that I said I should come to see him soon."

"I will not fail to do so, Monsieur."

"And you must forgive me for having been such a fool as to say anything to vex you. I can't imagine what I was thinking about, but when a man gets alone with such a pretty face, he is not always master of himself."

This remark, intended to convince the girl that he had meant nothing serious and there was an end of it, was not calculated to soothe her wounded vanity, but she accepted it meekly, as part of the disappointment destined for her, and responded in the same strain.

"There is nothing to forgive, Monsieur, I knew that it was only *badinage* on your part, but I shall never forget your kindness to me, nor cease to pray the Blessed Virgin to protect and keep you," and clasping for a moment the hand which Gordon Romilly extended to her, Véroniquė guided her cow into the homeward path, and parted from him.

He stood for a little time, watching the graceful figure, which, with one arm cast about the neck of "Erin," never turned to look at him again, and then, with a sigh, which really was heartfelt, he remounted his pony and rode him slowly back to the cantonment.

CHAPTER XIV.

GORDON ROMILLY'S DECISION.

As Gordon Romilly re-entered Ootacamund, everything appeared dull and changed to him. The sun was shining as brightly as when he left it; the carriage-drive about the lake was as full of moving figures; but he passed through them now, utterly regardless of their vicinity, or noticing it with a return of his old impatience. He hated the place, the people, their customs and costumes, as much as he had ever professed to do; and was only desirous to escape the sight of them as soon as possible, and bury himself and his disappointment in the privacy of his own room.

For he was more annoyed and disappointed than he chose to confess. His vanity, wounded at her unexpected rebuff, had induced him to speak lightly of his failure on parting with Véronique, but he did not think lightly of it, even in the first moments of their separation. He had imagined that the little country-bred girl would consider herself but too honoured by the proffer of his love, and accept it for just so long as it pleased him to bestow; that she was too simple and child-like in her ideas, in fact, to calculate what might be the end of such attentions on his part, and to find, therefore, that she was so horribly alive to the probable consequences, was a regular downfall for all Captain Romilly's hopes of amusement. Not, as has been said before, that he had any intention of deceiving Véronique; he was foolish and thoughtless, it is true, but he was too much of a gentleman to lay a fixed plan for a girl's destruction; yet he had anticipated flirting with her at the very least; and now that her common sense had laid a veto upon even that small diversion, Gordon Romilly became aware that he had anticipated a good deal more. Thinking over what she had said, and the serious air with which she had said it, the A.D.C. felt as though he had proposed to, and been rejected by her; and he called himself a fool, with an adjective attached to it, twenty times that evening, as he paced up and down his room, and wondered how he could have been so insane as to court an interest in a girl respecting whom her virtue precluded him from having light intentions, and her birth from entertaining serious ones. Why did he ever go and tumble over that precipice? and, having tumbled, why did he persist in remaining in bed, long after he might have left it with comfort to himself, so that he might retain the presence of Véronique about his pillow, and excite the sympathetic pity which she was so ready to give—knowing the peculiarity of his temperament, Captain Romilly would have added, only something rose up inwardly to tell him that his former experiences were no criterion for this one, and that he had never felt before what he felt now. The knowledge only made him stamp and rave the more.

He had permitted himself to fall in love —yes! actually to fall in love, there was no denying the fact, and he was quite sure he had made himself miserable for life by doing so—with a half-bred girl little more than a child, quite uneducated or versed in the ways of society, and, in point of birth and station, utterly beneath himself. But here his affection, which for the time was real, rose up to rebuke the charges he had brought against her, and the *piquante* attractive face of Véronique appeared as a background to his arguments, and put them to the rout. She was not half-bred; she was a thorough Irish girl, with the genuine Irish mixture of blue eyes and black hair; and the drop of foreign blood which she had inherited was only sufficient to make her more distractingly charming in his eyes. She was not uneducated; she was better informed, as her conversation proved, than half the ladies that he knew; and better bred, and more fit to grace an elevated station, than half the women who sat in high places at that very moment. He had libelled Véronique in saying what he did. She was an object as far removed from being made the plaything of a gentleman's leisure as from being made his wife. As Gordon Romilly uttered this truth to himself, he started.

"And why not his wife?" was the thought that ran rapidly through his brain; "why not *my* wife, as well as any other woman? once removed from this country and people, what is there in Véronique Moore that I should not be proud to own as belonging to myself?"

At the mere idea of thus possessing her, the young man felt his blood run quicker, and he could not but be aware therefrom how dangerous a notion it was for him to dwell on. For the next moment there rose up the image of his father, and of what he would say to the news of such a marriage. Captain Romilly had not forgotten his former peccadillo, nor the commotion it had caused at home. It had been slight compared to what this one would be, having never gone beyond a series of foolish letters to a pretty shop-girl, and a threatened action for breach of promise of marriage in consequence from her parent, but Lord Erskine Romilly's strictures on the occasion were well remembered by his son. He was surprised, he was astonished, he was hurt beyond measure, to find that a child of his, that a Romilly, that a grandson of the Earl of Bournemouth, that an officer in her Majesty's service, could so forget himself, lower himself, disgrace himself, and injure himself, as to make love to a woman of the plebeian classes.

He had thought better of him, hoped better of him, and expected better of him; and if such a thing ever occurred again, he should—stop his allowances, which was invariably the *summum bonum* of all Lord Erskine Romilly's lectures to his prodigal son. But as he had found from experience that it was the only method by which he could keep Master Gordon in anything like order, no one contemned the old lord for his oft-repeated threat except the subject of it, who considered it an unanswerable proof of the severity with which his father regarded his youthful indiscretions. Whether this were true or not, however, it had had the power as yet of keeping them within due bounds; and Captain Romilly knew that he could not afford to disregard it now. It was his foolish love-affair at Winchester which had been the means of transporting him to India as an A.D.C., for his father, afraid of trusting him any longer in the same town as his *inamorata*, under the usual threat of stoppage of allowances, had compelled him to accept the appointment he procured for him, thereby unwittingly casting his son from the frying-pan into the fire. But though undoubtedly scorched, Captain Romilly as yet showed no signs of burning himself. With one serious thought of Lord Erskine Romilly's anger, and consequent measures, should he hear of such an *escapade* on his part, he resolved it must not be—and tried to pooh-pooh the notion of such a marriage, as an excellent jest which he had raised for a moment's entertainment, but which in reality he was as far from contemplating as from stringing himself up to the bed-post. Finding, however, that the jest lingered about his memory, notwithstanding the many pipes he smoked, and the many "brandies and sodas" he imbibed in order to exorcise it, longer and more perseveringly than he found pleasant, Gordon Romilly broke through the reserve he had hitherto maintained towards the members of the Ootacamund Club, and, stepping from his lofty pedestal, condescended to mix in their society, and join in their amusements.

He did not, to his misfortune, find a second Romer there (for the presence of his sensible and kind-hearted friend at this time might have been the saving of him), but there were several liberal-minded gentlemen amongst them, who, taking in account the A.D.C.'s youth and evident bringing-up, consented to overlook his former haughty bearing, and make him welcome to their company.

But billiards, cards, and smoking, although excellent adjuncts to this life, when the rest of the stream runs smoothly, have no power to dam up the course of a torrent like interrupted love. Do what Captain Romilly would to distract his wayward fancy, the image of Véronique haunted it by night and by day, until, when nearly three weeks had elapsed from the time when he had parted from her, he was so tired of fighting with his own feelings, and so disheartened by his want of success, that he resolved to leave the hills again without seeing her, and go down to Madras to resume the duties of his appointment. With which end in view he was one evening bundling all his possessions pell-mell into his portmanteaux, when his native servant appeared at his bedroom door, to say that "the Roman priest" had asked to see him, and was waiting down below.

"Show him up!" cried Romilly, who, surrounded by articles of all sorts, was kneeling in shirt and trousers by the side of one of his travelling cases. "Tell him that I'm busy, and that if he wants to see me he must come up to my bedroom," which direction was followed in a few minutes by the entrance of Père Joseph in the black canonical robe in which he always paraded the cantonment.

"Monsieur, I fear that I disturb you!" he said as Captain Romilly rose from his position to greet him.

"Not at all, *mon père*," exclaimed the young officer with affected gaiety, for the sight of the priest recalled some of his most unpleasant recollections, "I am very glad to see you, only you must find yourself a chair to sit on. You see I am doing a little packing, preparatory to a move."

"Another shooting excursion, Monsieur?" asked Père Joseph with a smile.

"No, not exactly! I'm going to give over shooting for the present, and hand ladies in to dinner again instead. I return to Madras to-morrow!"

"So soon! I did not imagine your leave was so short—"

"No more it is; it has a month still to run, but I am sick of this place. There is nothing to do here, nothing to see, and no one to speak to—and it's so horribly healthy that there's not the least chance of a fellow's falling ill and getting sent back to England—so I consider that I am wasting my precious time; and am all impatience to get back to Madras and put my liver out of order that I may work up for an S.C."

"A strange desire, Monsieur, as some people would think, but everyone knows his own requirements best. Yet, as it happens so, I am doubly glad that I took the liberty of calling on you to-day, else I should have missed the pleasure of seeing you again."

"Oh! I daresay I should have found time to ride out to the bungalow between this and that," said Captain Romilly, who had intended studiously to avoid doing anything of the kind; but the priest, though he bowed courteously as if he believed him, did not take any further notice of the remark.

"I had occasion to come into Ootacamund this afternoon," he said, "to visit some of my flock, and not having seen you,

Monsieur, since you had the great kindness to send me your valuable present (though Véronique told me she had met you once upon the hills), I could not resist making an attempt to gain your presence, in order that I might thank you in person for the honour you conferred upon me."

"It is nothing—nothing!" said Captain Romilly, trying to waive the subject of the chair. "I trust that Mademoiselle is well?"

"I am sorry to say that I do not think she is well," replied Père Joseph, "Véronique has drooped visibly for some weeks past, but then she has had great cause to fret herself, Monsieur, and the mind generally re-acts upon the body."

At this Gordon Romilly stopped short in his employment, and coloured like a girl.

"What cause?" he asked quickly.

He thought, perhaps, that the priest had been questioning his niece on the subject of her failing looks, and drawing from her the reason of them, was there with the intention of taking him to task as the author and promoter of her melancholy.

But such an idea was the very farthest from Père Joseph's mind.

"I don't know why I should hesitate to tell you, Monsieur, who have shown so kind an interest in all that concerns us, but please to understand that it is to go no farther. You have seen the young native David, who lives with us," (Gordon Romilly nodded). "He has been to me, from his birth I may say (for he was only a few days old when I first found him), as a son, and to Véronique as a brother, and neither of us supposed, till lately, that he had ever cherished any thought or hope of becoming otherwise."

Here Captain Romilly threw down the boots and brushes with which he had armed himself, and taking his seat upon a pile of coats and trousers, turned an anxiously expectant face upon his visitor.

"Till within the last few weeks, Monsieur, as I was telling you, I have always imagined that David loved Véronique as a sister and nothing more."

"But surely he could never be so presumptuous!" interrupted the young officer hastily.

"Unfortunately for his own happiness, Monsieur, he is. Some trifling disagreement between my niece and himself, drew the truth from him, which came upon me and her as a thunder clap. So unexpected and hidden, indeed, was the intelligence that Véronique could in no wise bring herself to believe that he desired her for his wife; and the scene of distress which ensued was very trying, both to the girl and poor David. He being resolute in his insistance that she must have perceived his passion, and she in hers, that she had never dreamt of such a thing."

"As who would have done?" exclaimed Captain Romilly hotly, "they are as opposite as night and day."

"No one can be more aware of the difference between them, Monsieur, than my poor son," said Père Joseph quietly; "he is very humble in his love, he only desires that it should be known as such, and that it is ready to do all things for her. So, seeing how his presence and dumb distress upset my niece, I have sent David down to the plains, to spend a couple of months with my fellow labourer Père Michel at Coimbatore, for which he departed yesterday. And there, for the present, the matter rests. Whether it will never again be revived between them, or whether after a time Véronique may come to view his proposals in a different light, I cannot say, but—"

"But," interposed Gordon Romilly, who had risen to his feet with a face on fire, at the prospect presented to him, "you would surely never give your consent to such a sacrifice, *mon père*. You would never permit Véronique to marry a black—a native—a nigger? The very idea is too horrible to contemplate."

"Monsieur!" replied the priest, who evidently did not like the terms applied to his adopted son, "David may not be of the same blood or nation as ourselves, but he has a heart equal to that of any white man, and far superior to most. I have watched that lad from a little child, Monsieur; I know how noble and generous a nature his is, and although I would never force the inclination of Véronique in any direction, I should be ashamed of her did I think that her principal objection to this marriage lay in the colour of my poor boy's skin. A black skin, Monsieur, but a white soul! take my word for it; and a man likely to make the girl a better husband than nine-tenths of the Europeans she will meet out here. Besides, after all, should she finally reject the suit of David, for what is she reserved? Perhaps, to become the wife of a drunken soldier, or to sink still lower, who can tell? Monsieur, at times my heart is very heavy for Véronique: I see that she is well-favoured and admired; I know that I must soon leave her penniless and unprotected in this country, and I dread what may become of her, if she is not happily married beforehand. I cannot abandon her to become the prey of any lawless nature which she may meet; I would rather see her a wife, though against her own will!"

"*Mon père!* I will protect her against every possible danger. Give Véronique to me, and I will marry her to-morrow!"

If Gordon Romilly had drawn his pistols from the case beside him, and pointed their muzzles at Père Joseph's breast, he could not have more powerfully astonished him. The priest was so taken aback by the unexpected proposal, that he continued to stare in silent dismay, as though he feared that the gentleman before him had gone mad; whilst the A.D.C. in striving to make his meaning clearer, did not tend to re-establish the fact of his sanity, by the torrent of excited language which poured from his lips.

"Give her to me, Père Joseph, and I will marry her to-morrow—she is not fretting about David's suit, or any such rubbish, the darling! she is fretting about myself, and I know it as plainly as though she had told me; I said that I loved her, when I met her on the hills, but I did not say what

I know now, that it is impossible for me to live without her. I was going down to Madras to try what change of scene and place might do for me; but I know I should have been back here again in a couple of days, so I may as well save myself the journey. Only say I may have her, *mon père*, and I'll procure longer leave, or return to fetch her, or do anything you think fit, in order to make her my wife."

In his eagerness to secure the promise that Véronique should be his, Gordon Romilly had totally forgotten his father's anger, and its probable consequences; he had forgotten everything, in fact, except the fear that the girl whom he had honoured with his love, should be sacrificed to his dusky rival. He stood before Père Joseph, with a glowing face and extended arm, vowing and swearing as though he had no one in the world but himself to consult on the subject of his wishes or intentions.

"But stay! *mon fils*," said the priest, when he had a little recovered his intense surprise, " stay a minute, and let me fully understand what you are saying. If I have heard you aright, you love, or fancy that you love, my niece, and wish to make her your wife. This is a very startling and wonderful proposition to me, who have heard nothing of it up to this moment, but at the same time it cannot fail to be a very gratifying one. Yet, there is one important question to be first considered—what would your family say to such a marriage ?"

At this appeal Captain Romilly's face visibly lengthened. Hitherto he had ignored Lord Erskine Romilly's opinions on the subject, but he knew what they would be too well to continue to do so, when brought so palpably to his recollection ; so he stammered as he replied—

" I would marry Véronique directly, Père Joseph, as I said before, but I don't think I should venture all at once to make my marriage known to my family. They have certain prejudices and fancies, which I scorn to hold, and it might require a little time for preparation before I broke the news to them. But what difference can that make?"

Yet that it did make a difference Gordon Romilly soon perceived from the priest's continued silence and look of grave abstraction.

"See here, *mon père*," continued the young man, frankly, "I am of age, it is true, but I come of a noble family, and my father, Lord Erskine Romilly, has very high ideas about the woman whom I shall make my wife. At present I am dependent upon him for the best part of my income, and any act which he considered a dereliction of duty on my part, might cause him to withdraw his aid from me. But my father is an old man, who at his death must leave me a sufficient sum of money to make me independent, and even without that prospect I am rising in my profession every year, and shall soon be able to do without aid from anyone. Meanwhile, let me have Véronique for my wife, and when I leave this country, if my father still lives, and I stand in the army where I do at present, I will risk everything, both friends and fortune, in order to acknowledge her right to the station I shall have given her."

Still Père Joseph continued to look thoughtful.

"Your proposal is a very noble one, Monsieur, a very noble and a very generous one; and I think you must really be attached to Véronique to make it, but with all its promised advantages it is not to be accepted without due deliberation. You offer me the strongest temptation with which it is possible I should be assailed— the temptation of seeing my child make a marriage far above what even her worth or beauty could merit, or my highest ambition desire. Yet there is much to be said beforehand. Véronique is poor and lowly-born, and imperfectly educated, but she must not go to a man who will tire of her, or reproach her, or be ashamed of her!"

"Can you imagine I should be so base?" said Romilly, indignantly.

"No, Monsieur! I do not, but at present I can say no more about it. Her birth is so much beneath yours, that you must not act in the matter without a grave examination of your own feelings. At the same time, her virtue is so much above that of any man, that it is my part to see that it be not hastily thrown away. And, as yet, I am not even aware if the child loves you."

"Ask her!" exclaimed Captain Romilly, the light of expectation dancing in his eye, "take your answer from her own lips, *mon père*."

"I will do so, Monsieur, and meanwhile, this most sudden and unexpected proposal of yours has so upset me that I ask your permission to retire. I want to get home, that I may ponder deliberately over this important question, amidst the quiet of my own thoughts."

"And when may I follow you?" asked the young man, eagerly.

The old man smiled; such a smile as would almost have led one to believe that at some time he had experienced the same eagerness, and could feel for it.

"To-morrow evening, if you do not hear

from me, before, *mon fils*," he answered, laying his hand for a moment on Gordon Romilly's head; and with that he quitted the apartment, and left the A.D.C. to his own reflections.

CHAPTER XV.

HONEY VERSUS MONEY.

THE deed was done. Gordon Romilly had pledged his word that, always supposing she accepted him, he would marry Véronique Moore; and as a gentleman and a man of honour, it was impossible that he should now draw back. So he inwardly decided, as left to the cooling influences of solitude and silence, he sat down to calmly review what had passed between himself and Père Joseph.

Not that he repented of the promise which he had so rashly given; on the contrary, he was excited with pleasure as he reflected that in the delirium of the moment he had leapt the barrier, which he scarcely would have dared attempt by the light of common sense. It is true that he felt an occasional qualm of conscience as the thought of his father's anger, and the objections of the entire family, rose to his mind; but he salved it over, by remembering that the marriage was to be a private one, and that if it suited his convenience to keep it so for the next ten years, there was no one of sufficient influence to gainsay his decision. With his usual reckless disregard of consequences, Captain Romilly refused to look forward to all the *désagrémens* which must inevitably result from such an union. Véronique stood in the path before him, smiling, with extended arms, and he saw but that one image, and rushed forward, panting and breathless, to secure it, and had any other incentive been needed to spur him onward in his headlong course, it would have been amply supplied by a vision of the unfortunate David, now broiling beneath the sun of Coimbatore, but ready at any moment, on the field becoming clear, to return and walk over the course.

For the rest of the evening Captain Romilly indulged in the most extravagant spirits, whistling, singing and dancing about his room, whilst he turned all the contents of his portmanteau out upon the floor again, and flew from one occupation to another with the heedlessness of a boy who has gained an unexpected holiday, and does not know what to do in order to express his happiness. At the same time, it was difficult even for himself to say whether his gaiety were assumed or real. He anticipated what lay before him as much as it was possible for a man to do, but he had an uneasy sense the while of being about to take a great responsibility upon himself, and to promise more perhaps than he should be able to perform; and this uneasy sensation oppressed him, more or less, from that time forward, although he never admitted that he felt it, and usually carried it off with a vast amount of whistling and affected laughter.

Receiving no communication from Père Joseph on the following day, at about five o'clock he mounted his pony, and took the road to the priest's bungalow, glowing with the anticipation of falling into the arms of Véronique as soon as ever he arrived there. But in this hope he was disappointed, for as soon as the sound of his pony's hoofs was heard on the path outside the garden, Père Joseph himself appeared at the gate, and took the reins from him.

"Be good enough to walk inside, Monsieur," he said, "and take a seat, until I have put your pony in the stable," and when Captain Romilly had done as he desired him, he found that the room was vacant.

"Véronique! Véronique! my darling! come down to me!" he whispered loudly up the bedroom staircase, but no Véronique appeared in answer to his summons, and Père Joseph, catching him in the act, smiled at his discomfiture.

"She will not come down, Monsieur," he said, quietly, "until I give her leave. You must excuse me if I say that I cannot allow you to have any communication with her until you and I have had a little further talk together."

He motioned the A.D.C. to a chair, as he spoke, and Gordon Romilly sat down, burning with impatience, and in a mood to make any promises that might be required of him, so long as the coming interview were speedily concluded.

"Monsieur!" commenced the priest, who appeared most distractingly cool in the lover's impatient eyes, "the news which you conveyed to me yesterday has caused me a sleepless night."

"Very sorry to hear it, I'm sure!" exclaimed Captain Romilly, who was wondering inwardly what earthly difference that could make to him.

"Yes," resumed Père Joseph, "I came home, and I questioned Véronique, and discovered (more from her blushes and her silence than her words) that she was as well inclined towards your suit, Monsieur, as she is averse to that of poor David!"

"Didn't I tell you so?" interrupted the A.D.C., with a bright smile.

"Yes! it was not more than I expected, for who could think otherwise, with such a dazzling prospect opened to the child? But she is but a child, Monsieur, she completed her seventeenth year two months ago, and if she had not an older head to think for her, she might fall into all manner of trouble and distress. Before I let you see her, or proceed any further in this matter, therefore, I must understand fully what are your intentions regarding her."

"I told them to you yesterday," replied Romilly, rather curtly, for he feared that Père Joseph might be about to stipulate for a public marriage. "I can't marry your niece openly, nor acknowledge her as my wife just at present, because it would be the means of making me quarrel with my family; but I will marry her privately, if you will consent to my doing so, and she shall enjoy all the privileges of my name and station until she can publicly assume them. I cannot say more!"

"Some would say, Monsieur, that considering you are speaking of a soldier's daughter, you had already said too much; yet Véronique is too dear to me to be given to you on any other terms. But in what manner do you intend her to live after she shall have become your wife? I am content that she, for awhile, shall dispense with the glory of being acknowledged as such; but I could not consent to see her maiden name dishonoured, without the means of confuting any probable slander cast upon it for your sake."

"Do not be afraid for Véronique's name or reputation, *mon père*," said the young officer, gaily, "my wife's will be as dear to me as my own. I shall leave her on the Hills, either with yourself, or in any position that you may think most desirable; and I promise you that if at any time my visits to her shall prove a source of scandal, I will take her down to Madras with me at once, and acknowledge her as Mrs. Romilly."

At the mention of that name, the priest's breast heaved with gratified ambition, and all his remaining objections to the marriage faded beneath the influence of his master passion.

"It is enough, *mon fils*," he said, rising from his seat, "if you promise me that, I have nothing further to say. Véronique may well put up with a little privation and a little delay, for the sake of the brilliant future which opens before her. But you have still to ask her own opinion on the subject," he added, smiling, "and I will not therefore keep her from you, longer."

He walked to the foot of the staircase, calling "Véronique!" and then he turned to leave the room.

"She will not keep you waiting, Monsieur," he said with a gentle inclination of the head, "and meanwhile I will attend to the wants of your pony. Since my poor lad's departure, the care of the cattle has devolved upon myself," with which words Père Joseph passed into the verandah, and Gordon Romilly took up the station he had vacated at the bottom of the staircase. In another moment, she was before him. In another moment, the door which led from the upper storey was flung open, and Véronique in holiday costume, with red ribbons twisted in her black plaits of hair, had set her foot upon the staircase, and meeting the glowing, ardent glance directed upwards to attend her coming, stood there, blushing and trembling from head to foot, too bashful to advance, and too delighted to retreat.

"Come here, Véronique," said Gordon Romilly, holding out his arms to receive her, "come here, and tell me, if you'll be my little wife!"

"*Votre femme,*" exclaimed the girl, without moving from her position, "*Monsieur! c'est impossible, je ne peux pas le croire.*"

"Say that it shall be so, Véronique, and I'll soon make you believe it! But, perhaps, you would rather not?"

"Monsieur!" in a tone of remonstrance.

"Well, come down here then, and tell me what you wish." She advanced a few steps timidly towards him, and he put out his hand and pulled her down the remainder of the flight, until she rested in the circle of his embrace.

"Will you marry me, Véronique?" kissing her.

"*Mais oui, Monsieur.*"

"Will you be my wife?" kissing her again.

"*Mais oui, Monsieur.*"

"Will you ever call me 'Monsieur' again?"

"*Mais oui, Monsieur,*" replied Véronique, not knowing what she said, in her coy struggles to escape from the vehement embraces which frightened rather than assured her. "*Sainte Mère de Dieu! je vous benis pour toutes vos bontés,*" murmured the girl with uplifted eyes, as Gordon Romilly at last released her from his arms, and she could sufficiently collect her agitated thoughts to remember the good fortune which had fallen upon her. As she uttered her simple prayer the little Christian turned towards the *bénitier*, and solemnly crossing herself with its holy water, laid her wet fingers lightly upon Romilly's forehead.

"*Ah! que je suis heureuse que vous êtes

chrétien, Monsieur Gor-don," she exclaimed joyfully, "*fussiez-vous resté un hérétique, notre mariage eût été impossible!*"

But what was her surprise at the conclusion of this innocent speech, to see her lover, who had had his eager gaze fixed upon her face at the commencement, turn suddenly from the staircase and herself, and walk away to take up a position by the window which looked into the garden. Véronique could not imagine what had happened to disturb him, but she was too shy and too little familiar with Captain Romilly to demand an immediate explanation. So she only ventured to follow as far as the table, and to stand there in silent expectation, whilst she regarded the back of his figure with her wistful eyes. Meanwhile, his thoughts were in such a whirl that he hardly remembered where he was, nor how strange his conduct must appear to her, for her words had struck his conscience like a voice from heaven. Since the time that he had contemplated marrying Véronique Moore, until that moment, he had never once thought of the difference in their religion, nor of the difficulties that fact must throw in the way of a private union. To wed her as a Roman Catholic, in the little chapel beside which he stood, and with her uncle as officiating priest, would be easy enough, but to have a second ceremony performed in the Protestant church at Ootacamund, would be to render the business patent to all India. It was impossible; it was not to be thought of; he must go at once, and however unpleasant for himself, confess to Père Joseph the folly of which he had been guilty in concealing the truth respecting his religion, and point out to him the obstacles it would throw in the furtherance of the plan which they had agreed upon.

"*Ai-je dit quelque chose pour vous déplaire?*" enquired the gentle voice of Véronique, by his side, and Gordon Romilly started from his reverie to see two tender blue eyes, moistened with the fear of his displeasure, and two rosy parted lips, quivering with suppressed emotion. All his ideas changed at the sight. She loved him, and he had promised to marry her, and the powers of darkness should not wrest her from him now.

"No, my darling!" he replied, fervently, as he opened his arms again, and took the slight form into his embrace, "a sudden thought struck me that I am not worthy enough to be your husband, but if you will take me as I am, Véronique, with all my sins upon my head, I'll cleave to you as fast and firmly as any other man."

He said this, thinking to himself the while, that the Roman Catholic ceremony should be as binding on him as though he were of the same faith as herself; and that when he acknowledged her as his wife before all the world, he would marry her over again in his own church, and silence her scruples for evermore. It did not take much trouble on his part to reassure Véronique's trembling fears, nor to make her light happy laugh ring through the little bungalow again; and Gordon Romilly wished that he could as easily have shaken off the gloom which oppressed himself, whenever he thought of the deception he had practised on her, or heard the allusions made by Père Joseph or his niece, to the religion which they supposed to be common to all three.

He was moody and silent for the remainder of the evening, and his manner would have excited suspicion in any one less simple than the priest, or less trusting than Véronique; but he turned off their kind enquiries as to the cause with the convenient plea of headache, and, on the promise of returning on the morrow, rose early to take his leave.

It was Véronique who, despite all his protestations, fetched his pony from the stable this time, and it was Véronique who stood in the moonlight by the garden gate to see her gallant lover ride away.

"Good-night, my pretty one!" said Gordon Romilly, trying to speak cheerfully in order to atone for his late gloom.

"*Bon soir,*" she whispered, "*et que Dieu te garde!*"

"But you must learn to talk English now, my darling, that you have promised to become an Englishman's wife," said the young officer in reply; "you must drop that habit of falling back on French every second minute, or I shan't believe that I have married an Irish girl."

She smiled at this rebuke, and repeated her sentence.

"Good-night, Monsieur, and take good care of yourself."

"Good-night—what?" bending from his saddle-bow to catch her half-murmured words; but Véronique, conscious of what she had said, was too much ashamed to repeat it.

"Call me by my proper name," said Romilly imperatively, "without any Monsieur attached to it at all;" and the coming lordship seemed to cast its shadow on her beforehand, for she obeyed him without hesitation—

"Good-night, *Gordon, mon bien-aimé!*"

The tone in which she uttered these words was so fervent that Captain Romilly lifted up the pretty face caressingly laid against his saddle-bow, and regarded it earnestly.

"Do you love me then so much, Véronique?"

"*Gor-don, tu le sais*," she answered, and her glowing eyes met his, and mingled with them. He dropped the hand with which he had upheld her face, and heaved a sigh.

"Good-night, then, Véronique; good-night, and don't forget to pray that I may make as good a husband as you deserve to have," and with that he rode away on the moonlit path, and left her standing by the gate alone. As he did so, his heart was full of trouble and confusion. He knew that he was going to do a wrong thing, and his principles were just correct enough to forbid his doing it without compunction, whilst they were not of sufficient force to prevent his doing it at all. He was quite ready to admit that in the eyes of the law he had no right to marry Véronique Moore as a Roman Catholic; at the same time he argued that the marriage would be quite as much a marriage in the eyes of Heaven, and therefore, whilst he adhered to the obligations incurred by it, he should not sin. And to strengthen this decision came the thought of Véronique's love, and of her disappointment if he failed to keep his word ; and, after all, as he said to himself, he could at any moment marry her over again according to the rites of the Protestant church, and put the matter straight. He intended to inform her of his own faith as soon as she should be irrevocably his ; and to trust to her affection to pardon him for the deception practised on her.

Meanwhile it must be one of two things, either he must be united to Véronique under her present belief, or not at all, for a wedding at Ootacamund was not to be contemplated for a moment. And, reasoning thus to suit his own convenience, Captain Romilly arrived at the conclusion that his first intentions must hold good, for to surrender his hopes of possessing the sparkling, fascinating girl who had shown him so much of her heart that evening was, in his estimation, a calamity not to be borne.

So he quieted his conscience as best he might, although it pricked him, not only then, but many a time afterwards, when the old priest, in his anxiety to discover the state of mind of his future nephew, probed him with queries on the subject of religion, from which he could barely escape with truth.

The days went on, and before a week had elapsed all the preliminaries necessary for the simple marriage had been arranged. As the ceremony was to be kept a strict secret, not only from Romilly's friends, but from David himself, it was agreed that the bridegroom should leave Ootacamund, as for a shooting excursion, and go and spend a fortnight at the priest's bungalow instead. To this end he dispatched his native attendants and Arab horse (which by this time had quite recovered its lameness) down to Bandypoor the day before, with orders to remain there until they heard from him, and casually giving out that he expected to be absent for some time on a trip into the jungle, bade farewell to his acquaintances at the club, and rode away on his Pegu to the place of appointment.

As it was necessary that there should be witnesses to the nuptials, Père Joseph procured the assistance of some of his native converts, who lived still further from the Cantonment than he did, and, speaking no English, were not likely to blab the secret to any one of importance ; and thus, one morning, surrounded by three or four East Indians, alone, Gordon Romilly received the hand of Véronique Moore from her uncle, and made her, to all intents and purposes, his wife. When the hour really arrived, he was too happy and elated to permit the illegality of the ceremony to disturb his bliss ; and, notwithstanding all his former fickleness, notwithstanding his present deception, and the gloom in which his future actions were enveloped, Gordon Romilly's heart beat as truly towards Véronique on the day he married her as ever bridegroom's beat towards his bride.

He did not love her as well or as faithfully, perhaps, as some men can love; but he loved her as passionately as it was in his nature to do. And as Véronique, in her guileless innocence of love or its requirements, had no magic charm by which to gauge the depths of his affection, she also, for the time being, was supremely blest.

END OF VOL. I.

BILLING, PRINTER, GUILDFORD.

www.ingramcontent.com/pod-product-compliance
Lightning Source LLC
Chambersburg PA
CBHW021159230426
43667CB00006B/477